The Shaping of Prophecy

The Shaping of Prophecy

Passion, Perception and Practicality

ADRIAN HASTINGS

GEOFFREY
CHAPMAN

Geoffrey Chapman
A Cassell imprint
Wellington House, 125 Strand, London WC2R 0BB
215 Park Avenue South, New York, NY 10003

First published 1995

British Library Cataloguing-in-Publication Data
A catalogue record for this book is available from the British Library.

ISBN 0-225-66776-2

Typeset by Create Publishing Services
Printed and bound in Great Britain by Biddles Ltd, Guildford and King's Lynn

Contents

For

DONALD NICHOLL
friend of fifty years

and

in memory of

DONALD LIDDELL
died in Normandy, June 1944
pacifist, parachutist and stretcher-bearer

Acknowledgements

Chapter 1 first appeared in the *University of Leeds Review* for 1994; chapter 3 was printed as a *Milton Keynes and Malvern Paper*, June 1994; a much reduced version of chapter 4 appeared in the *Times Higher Educational Supplement*, 7 September 1990; chapter 5 was published in Geoffrey Rowell (ed.) *The English Religious Tradition and the Genius of Anglicanism*, Ikon, 1992, 211–26; chapter 6 in Adrian Hastings (ed.) *Bishops and Writers*, Anthony Clarke, 1977, 107–26; chapter 7 in Andrew Morton (ed.) *God's Will in a Time of Crisis: A Colloquium Celebrating the 50th Anniversary of the Baillie Commission*, CTPI, University of Edinburgh, 1994, 4–13; chapter 8 in *One in Christ*, 1993.1, 65–75; chapter 9 in *Theology*, May/June 1992, 163–76; chapter 12 in the *Tablet*, 8 August 1992, the *Guardian* 3 July 1993 and *Theology*, July/August 1994, 242–4; chapter 15 in the *Tablet*, 22/29 December 1990.

* * *

Two friends have made this book's completion possible, just as I was approaching the moment of academic retirement. Without the insistent encouragement of Ruth McCurry, it would not even have been imagined in the form it has acquired. Without the ceaseless willingness of Ingrid Lawrie to type and revise its every part, it would never actually have existed.

Introductory

Introduction

The point, remarked Karl Marx, is not so much to interpret the world as to change it. Can we, however, hope to change it for the better unless we understand it? I remember sometimes being told, twenty years ago, by left-wing Catholic friends that while we did not share the underlying philosophy of Marxism, in so far as it was atheist, we should accept the 'Marxist analysis' as correct. It never seemed to me that it was: at least not wholly correct. I found it too simple. Forty years ago, when I was preparing to be ordained in Rome I had more or less to take it for granted that the Catholic, papal, analysis was correct, or, at least, accept in the nice words of an old Catholic Evidence Guild song, 'The Pope who is infallible and seldom goes far wrong'. Yet, even then, I was learning in the hard school of history how often popes had gone very wrong. It was, nevertheless, somewhat later that I first encountered that fascinating letter from Pope Gregory II to St Boniface, written in November 726. Boniface, busy establishing the church in Germany, had consulted the Pope about various moral problems, matters no less urgent then than population control and contraception, for instance, are now. Pope Gregory's answer deserves to be a great deal better known than it is:

> In (your) report you included a number of questions concerning the faith and teaching of the Holy Roman and Apostolic Church ... Since you seek our advice on matters dealing with ecclesiastical discipline, we will state with all the authority of apostolic tradition what you must hold, though we speak not from our own insufficiency but relying on the grace of him who opens the mouths of the dumb and makes eloquent the tongues of babes ...
>
> As to what a man shall do if his wife is unable through illness to allow him his marital rights, it would be better if he remained apart and practised continence. But since this is practicable only in the

case of men of high ideals, the best course if he is unable to be continent would be for him to marry. Nevertheless he should continue to support the woman who is sick, unless she has contracted the disease through her own fault ...

You ask further: if a father or mother gives a child during its early years to a monastery to be brought up in monastic discipline, is it lawful for that child, after reaching the age of puberty, to leave the cloister and enter matrimony? This we strictly forbid, for it is an impious thing to allow children who have been offered to God by their parents to follow their baser instincts for pleasure ... This, my dear brother, is all that needs to be said with the authority of the Apostolic See.

The seriousness of this teaching cannot be questioned. It was given by the most outstanding pope of his century. Nothing is more important than guidance given during the founding of a new church and this particular guidance was given with about as much stress on papal authority as Gregory could manage. He declared explicitly that he was witnessing to 'the faith and teaching of the Holy Roman and Apostolic Church'. He spoke, as he insisted, 'with the authority of the Apostolic See' and 'not from our own insufficiency'. Yet his teaching permitted bigamy in certain circumstances while the instructions about children dedicated to God in their infancy in a monastery are, to say the least, hardly reconcilable with subsequent church teaching on freedom and the right to marry.

We have here one of the many cases of authoritative papal teaching which have been, and are, simply erroneous and, indeed, immoral. Gregory II was no less pope than John Paul II is today. *Veritatis Splendor*, for instance, has no more claim *ipso facto* of its publication to be correct than Gregory II's letter. It is, as a matter of simple fact, part of Catholic history and therefore of good Catholic theology too that the pope is highly fallible. 'Get behind me, Satan! Because the way you think is not God's way but man's'; Jesus' rebuke to Simon Peter recorded by both Matthew and Mark, is a warning too seldom regarded but it is one that both popes and Christians in general should bear in mind. If the pope is, in some sense, Peter – and such remains the central claim of Rome – then a good deal of space needs to be found in any theology of the papacy for those very sharp words of Jesus. Papal teaching may far from represent the mind of God. It is most likely to be reliable and Spirit-inspired when it is prayerful, humble, conciliar and rational. That is what we learnt from the practice, as well as the teaching, of the Second Vatican Council. The pope has, however, no automatic ability to tap in on truth, the Holy Spirit or the correct moral options the world needs today. The more autocratic he is, the less collegial, the more likely he is to be both mistaken and misleading. He may be a prophet or he may not.

Again, we will certainly not find clear and reliable guidance for today's moral problems by simply opening the pages of a Bible. Fundamentalism is neither prophetic nor reliable. The appalling and dangerous rubbish deriving from its inspiration can never have been more obvious than in the message being purveyed by the latest wave of evangelical fundamentalists and the weirdly misplaced 'gospel of prosperity' they carry around the third world. One could go on and on listing the false teachers of today, from Marxists to monetarists and post-modernists. When serving in the University of Zimbabwe I was struck by how similar in its irrational certainty was the 'fundamentalism' of various of my Marxist colleagues with the fundamentalism of many Islamic and Christian Evangelical teachers. Catholicism seldom breeds so starkly irrational a cast of mind but, of course, once it effectively departs from the reiterated principle of Thomas Aquinas that grace does not destroy but perfect nature and faith does not contradict reason, it is only too prone to fall into the same large category.

Yet we do need moral guidance, teaching, skilful help in the understanding of a perplexing and increasingly dangerous world. We cannot get it infallibly from anyone and we hardly get it at all from the shallow rhetoric of our political and economic masters. Even academics now rather seldom venture forth from their increasingly restricted areas of specialisation to make publicly the wider connections needed if society as a whole is to be the subject of a critique in terms of truth, morality and honesty. Do such values even still exist? The gospel of post-modernism, to which many anti-fundamentalists are now succumbing, would deny it. No objectivity whatsoever is reachable behind the multitude of discordant human 'discourses'. Every medium is inherently subjective and every message is controlled by its medium. It is absolutely vital for the intellectual health and indeed the survival of sanity in our society that this sophisticated pessimism too be rejected. Despite the necessity of being suspicious about the distorting effect of privilege, class interest and the rest upon every 'message', every interpretation of history, every judgement upon the state of contemporary society, we do nevertheless retain the certainty that some interpretations, some judgements, are far more one-sided and distorting than others. This can only be so because there is in principle available to us an objectivity of truth and goodness.

It seems at times as if journalists have been left almost alone to carry this fearful responsibility of credibly evaluating the present and a few do it rather well, but as a group they have neither the detachment nor the longer view. Prophecy is an old-fashioned concept, biblically grounded. It evaluates the present in terms of absolutes, that is to say the sort of terms that we believe come nearest in our human conversation to the mind and judgement of the unknowable God. But the prophet is not a medium or diviner, an unthinking carrier of the words of a power possessing him. He does not claim infallibility. Like a good pudding, he can only be appraised in the eating. While attempting to express across the limitations of a particular human mind, a view of the contemporary world in terms of what is true, what is good, what really matters, what deserves today a commitment no less than passionate, prophecy accepts that it can only begin to do that if it includes two essential elements.

The first is as clear a rational and sophisticated understanding of the world as one can come to, an understanding historical, sociological, psychological. There is absolutely no short cut for pope, prime minister or professor to getting down to the analysis, closely focused, objective yet imaginative of the complex subtleties of our human history and present predicament. Without this, no one can speak with any sort of authority about what human society should now do in regard to this or that. The second remains fidelity to a tradition, a faith, a shared discourse out of which one speaks; not a rigid, uncritical fidelity but still the acceptance of a language and culture of meaning and of value; not just a shared subjectivity but a well-tried road opening on to the realism of an objective knowledge of things. For me that remains the central biblical, Christian and Catholic tradition. Despite its uncertainties, confusions and numerous overconfident simplicities, it remains, I believe, the best, most enduring, most truthful and usable, most divine of human belief systems.

The essays in this volume have been written for a variety of particular occasions, mostly since 1990. They focus on specific topics, some more methodological, some more historical, some essentially topical. They were not composed with any particular intention of being prophetic but they do provide something of a rounded but also frequently passionate approach to how one can be a human being with a Christian orientation in the world of the 1990s. Collectively these essays veer between the academic, the pastoral, the political, but they share a concern for the moral analysis of society; and that, for our modern needs, may fairly be described as prophecy.

1

Is Passion Needed for Perception?

Towards the end of *A Midsummer Night's Dream*, Theseus, the Duke of Athens, makes a marvellous comparison between the lunatic, the lover and the poet. What links the three is, it seems, a quality of imaginative passion that enables each to 'apprehend more than cool reason ever comprehends ...' Theseus fairly enough warns of the dangers of the 'tricks' produced by a strong imagination. The lunatic's passion may create a complex medley of images offering at times an almost intoxicating appeal to others but not leading to a real comprehension of anything at all: 'How easy is a bush supposed a bear!' Yet one sees in Blake, one of the most passionate of English poets, how close insight can come to lunacy, how impossible it can be quite to separate the two, but how infinitely poorer we would be without such enchantments. Both the poet and the lover fashion new eyes. A passionate love of a person, a place or a subject enables one to see things hitherto completely hidden.

That is true of one's mental entry into whole cultures. Cross-cultural perception, the leap of sensitivity allowing one to enter affectionately, and after that comprehendingly, into a culture, a way of thinking and being other than one's own, seems almost impossible without qualities of the heart quite as much as of the head. If one asks how as an anthropologist of genius Edward Evans-Pritchard could get as far as he did with Zande magic or Nuer religion, the answer must lie – far more, I think, than his critics have recognised – in his great ability to love Azande and Nuer. The ability to drop one's own being to become one with something other is a matter of the heart opening the door for the mind. It is, to speak symbolically, a process of dying and of rising again. A heightening of this process is what, theologically, is intended by kenosis, the emptying of divinity in the Son's adoption of humanity. That 'emptying' of which Paul speaks in the Epistle to the Philippians in relation to Jesus Christ's adopting the 'form of a servant' in place of 'the form of God' only ends with 'death on a cross'. This exercise of incarnation and self-emptying is, most certainly, one in communication. The Word of God's bold endeavour to be man, intelligible to humankind, is unimaginable without the element of passion. Divinity could not have demonstrated its willingness to understand from within what it meant to be human without the experience of emotion, rejection, even crucifixion. And without all of that we could never have received the word of revelation which it was intended to convey. So strange an intellectual exchange could not conceivably be effected on the level of intellect alone. It required a shared identity of affective experience. The Word was made flesh and dwelt among us and we saw his glory, a glory of truth, the fourth gospel tells us, but the seeing hardly begins before the anguish of the passion has been passed through. 'You cannot bear now what I have to tell you,' Jesus admitted. Cross, betrayal, a great many tears and a great deal of thinking would have to come first. In due course the Spirit of Truth would make it possible to begin to understand what the whole thing had been about, a process never ending.

Grace is never unlike nature, Thomas Aquinas consistently assures us. Karl Barth did not like him for it, but I do. The way in which revealed truth is brought in Christ to human minds should be a key to the way other truths are discovered and appropriated. As we move back and forth between the revealed and the natural, we do not forget Theseus' warning about the 'tricks' and fantasies passion may produce beyond the sphere of cool reason, but Shakespeare cannot have meant to belittle the achievement of the lover and the poet, for that, after all, is what *A Midsummer Night's Dream* is all about, while its interplay between fairies and humans is no bad metaphor for one between grace and nature. The relations between such kingdoms of the imagination may playfully insinuate the kingdoms of faith.

The passion of the *Dream* is all the same the passion of a first night. It can be the starting point, but no more, for a long trail of exploration as to how, on the one hand, passion takes one inexorably on through both pleasure and pain to birth and rebirth, while, on the other hand, it is a major constituent within the business of knowing. The passion of Christ was the culmination of a great love: 'Jerusalem, Jerusalem, how often would I have gathered your children together as a hen gathers her brood under her wings, and you would not!' (Matthew 23:37) and he wept over the city. While the fictional Nineveh of Jonah listened to the message, real cities seldom listen so willingly to real prophets. The process of perceiving and publicly communicating a truth that greatly matters seems inconceivable without intense criticism, conflict, the torment of a self-questioning mind. The Christ experience is one of a passionate self-giving which the Christian tradition presents as the epic not only of the Word of God but also of the Son of Man, the New Adam, a reconstituted humanity, Langland's Piers Plowman who combines in his person both what God has done for us and what a good man should be ready to do, the way truth, love and an intensity of human experience have to be held together in the career of every Piers Plowman, every citizen of Athens. What has Athens to do with Jerusalem? Tertullian once asked. The answer here is, just everything. The one is the other.

The Dinka of the southern Sudan may not appear to have much to do with either Athens or Jerusalem, but I would want to claim that both Athens and Jerusalem would be diminished if they could not find room within their walls for these Nilotes. The Dinka Masters of the Fishing Spear, as described by Godfrey Lienhardt in his superb ethnographic study *Divinity and Experience*, were their priests and prophets, men bearing the central human task of 'lighting the way', pronouncing and defining truth, reconciling the contentious and prevailing in prayer. Would we define those tasks as sacerdotal or political or academic? Something of all three, much as Gladstone or Thomas More or Cardinal Richelieu could combine something of the three; and it would be a self-inflicted wound if our own society insisted on dividing such functions too sharply.

The mythical originating Spear Master, Aiwel Longa, fused the powers of death and life. Indeed without the one you can hardly be imagined as possessing the other. Upon the Spear Master depends the life of the people, and the mystical strength of the Spear Master lies in the divinity, Flesh, pulsating within his body and at important ceremonies bringing him to partial dissociation. There is no doubt about the passionate character of a Spear Master and yet the Dinka stress still more the quality of coolness. The great Spear Master has a biting power to his prayer, comparable to the character of hot and bitter things, yet the bite is one that cuts through to the truth; it is an ability to judge accurately, an ultimate coolness of mind. It is for this that he is appreciated and that coolness continues to the end in the extraordinary events whereby some of the greatest of Spear Masters chose to die for the life of their people, lying in the grave, giving from there the last instructions and then, when finally silent, buried alive. The passion of the Spear Master is consummated in a great coolness within a total perception of his relationship to his people.

The dynamics of perception depend, I am suggesting, upon a correct interaction of heat and coolness. One of Robert Runcie's best sermons is entitled 'Passionate Coolness'. In it he explores the interplay of the passionate and the cool and that is what I want to do now. A central dilemma in human perception is that it seems so almost impossibly hard to break out of the conventionalities of any given mental world without a quality of near-irrational passion which all the same so easily rends askew the very perceptions reached. The impact of Marxism upon modern historical and political studies, both in the new, quite transforming, insights it offered and in the devastating skewing it produced, is now a matter of history which we can look back on with some detachment. It could never have happened without a large measure of Marxist passion not unlike the contemporary excitements of post-modernism. If we think back to creative visionaries like Blake, Dostoievski or Simone Weil, we can be both entranced and appalled by the power and consequences of their passion: so subtly perceptive in some things, so dangerously, madly, wrong in others. There seems a kind of spiritual and moral truth, immeasurably valuable, yet unattainable except through drinking of a chalice whose wine too easily spins dreams eschatological and wild. We would profoundly fail to interpret Jesus aright if we refused to locate him and his sayings in part within that almost mad wisdom where the human psyche experiences the divine at its most unsettling and contradictory and utopian. 'Leave the dead to bury the dead.' 'If anyone forces you to go one mile, go with him two miles.'

Passion is not irrelevant for academic life. The whole understanding the university seeks, or should seek, is one about humanity and the relationship of humanity to total reality, a relationship which if not inherently moral is sure to be disastrous. It can be a function of academic passion to ensure that the university retains the integrity to prefer the true and the good to the utilitarian and the profitable, to participate rationally and morally in the wholeness of a fully humane enterprise. That may seem a romantic and utopian conception, but by walking straight down a neatly defined path with guidelines for academic staff appraisal in one hand and a bottle of mineral water in the other, we won't necessarily achieve even our more mundane aspirations. A book of poetry and a bottle of wine may actually serve better if you want a 5 rating for your research output but, still more, if you want your academic production genuinely to contribute to the enhancement of human perception. If and when the cry 'Eureka' suddenly bursts from your lips, it will as likely as not have come, in Hopkins' words, from a 'tormented mind'.

> O the mind, mind has mountains: cliffs of fall
> Frightful, sheer, no-man-fathomed.

What, to turn to his greatest masterpiece, is *The Wreck of the Deutschland* but a 'Eureka' of exceptional perceptiveness into the meaning of God and disaster and death and hope, dragged out from the passion not only of the drowned nuns themselves but that of Hopkins and of Christ? Passion is, one may note, a recurring word through the poem. Again, if Hopkins' later poetry seems more often about a sense of crushing weariness which does not provide 'one rapture of an inspiration', the truth is that we do come here too, again and again, to incomparable richness the other side of pain as in the quite extraordinary power of resurrection affirmation in *That Nature is a Heraclitean Fire and of the Comfort of the Resurrection.* Or read the very rough and little known *Epithalamion*, still incomplete when he died, a description of wood and river and boys bathing in it, all to form part of a gloriously rich symbolic tribute to wedlock.

Passion may tend to the irrational. One cannot deny that it can cloud the judgement and make us take foolish decisions. Harness passion less to love than to sex, less to the commonwealth of freedom and pluralist tolerance than to nationalism, racism and Fascism, less to God than to some introverted messianic cult, and it will foster great silliness and great nastiness. And this happens often enough. We rightly use the word 'dispassionate' to refer to a particularly valuable quality of mind. The university is not immune to such follies and a certain detached coldness in academic style is one defensible form of response. Too passionate a commitment to a certain line in research can affect the objectivity with which one looks at evidence. There are at times painful examples which come to public notice when this has got quite out of hand, but most of us in our own work must be aware often enough of the danger of a too passionate, excited attachment to a particular thesis or hypothesis, and the danger of playing up examples which illustrate it, undercutting the significance of negative instances. Yet without an almost romantic commitment to hypotheses, hunch beliefs which we know are unproven but around which we organise our work, few of us would actually undertake any creative study at all. The long-term danger lies far less in the passion that we bring to our work than in pretending it is not there, in not recognising that in all sides of intellectual life commitment to a vision of things deriving largely from the heart has to run ahead of rationality, without running away from rationality.

Donald MacKinnon, probably the most influential philosophical theologian Britain has produced this century, died recently. An Oxford philosopher, he returned to Scotland as Regius Professor of Moral Philosophy in the University of Aberdeen before becoming in 1960 Norris-Hulse Professor of Divinity at Cambridge. Donald was a theologian entirely unwilling to separate the most intense intellectual rigour from a quite exceptional and passionate commitment to the wholeness of a moral reality which is always broken, tragic, intensely complex but not something the academic can stand back from. In his last letter to me, written on Ash Wednesday just a fortnight before his death, he referred to 'the longest letter I have ever had published in a newspaper – the *Scotsman!*' It was in criticism of Eden at the time of Suez. That was certainly passionate and I share his conviction that writing long letters to newspapers is one very appropriate way of expression for academic passion. Passion is needed both to fuel the research task itself to leap beyond the proven and to bend the eye of the academic back to the practical and the political, to compel the Regius Professor to write letters to the *Scotsman* about Suez. That passionate concern for the world outside the campus was what made Bertrand Russell or E. P. Thompson so influential precisely as intellectuals, just as it made MacKinnon so special. Perhaps academically it also marginalised all three, yet I hope Thompson's expression of passion about CND and much else was part of the reason why this university chose to offer him a doctorate in 1993, though, sadly, he died before he could receive it.

I too was opposed to Suez, deeply opposed, but it saddens me that in the 1990s there is so much less academic passion about Bosnia than there was, in the 1950s, about Suez. Yet the ground for outrage about the one is far greater than that of the other. Are the huge departments of politics present throughout Britain really doing their job if the academic community feels so little passion about the resurgence in Europe of nationalist aggression and attempted genocide fifty years after the 'Never Again' of the Holocaust?

We can, I believe, find passion too in the lives of the greatest scientists, in a Faraday or a Newton. 'Our subjects are so glorious,' wrote Faraday in 1854, 'that to work at them rejoices and encourages the feeblest; delights and enchants the strongest.' How is one to be swept along creatively by such enchantment yet not swept off course by the 'seething brains' and 'shaping fantasies' of Theseus' warning? Nothing is more memorable in the extraordinary cycle of the stories of Elijah than his experience of the word of the Lord on Mount Horeb. 'Go forth and stand upon the mount before the Lord,' he was told.

> And behold the Lord passed by, and a great and strong wind rent the mountains, and broke in pieces the rocks before the Lord, but the Lord was not in the wind; and after the wind an earthquake, but the Lord was not in the earthquake; and after the earthquake a fire, but the Lord was not in the fire; and after the fire a still small voice. And when Elijah heard it, he wrapped his face in his mantle and went out and stood at the entrance of the cave.   (I Kings 19.11–12)

The turmoil absolutely must come first, the story seems to be saying, but it is afterwards, all passion spent, that the word of truth comes through, and in the coolness of the still small voice the prophet and the academic can perceive truth, less dispassionately than post-passionately. That too may be the message of Passion Sunday. The agony in the garden passed, Jesus is portrayed in the gospels as extraordinarily cool, able to discuss the nature of truth with Pilate almost academically, still pastorally concerned at the end on Golgotha with weeping women and the man crucified beside him. Neither passion nor science enables us to master the whole of things, and together they still do not do so, yet each reins in the weaknesses of the other in the tricky business of perception. Communities in which either is banished are very wild or very arid. There is, I believe, more than ever a danger in the modern university of leaving no room for all those things not open to a very pedestrian assessment. If that should happen, the university of the future will be grievously maimed. The threat we face is not that polytechnics have become universities but that universities become polytechnics where letters may not be written to the press, beliefs be argued or students demonstrate, where passion will be excluded. On Passion Sunday in a university church let us pray that this may never be.

University of Leeds sermon,
Passion Sunday, 20 March 1994

2

Between Prayer and Politics
On Being a Christian Today

Being a Christian is inevitably a complex, varied and intensely individual matter. While the interacting relationship of prayer and politics remains only one side of it, I will try to show why this relationship is inherently so central to the art of being a Christian. Why, moreover, it is particularly crucial in our age, the 'today' we so often like to add rather glibly to our statements and queries about the significance of things. Post-Socialist, post-Communist, even post-Thatcherite, we will portray it as an intellectually and politically anarchic age, an age in which the message of a fashionable post-modernism appears to be that, if appropriately formulated, then anything goes: a do-it-yourself world in which there are no absolutes, no ultimates, no over-arching communion of meaning across nations and ages, only an endless series of discourses, each to be located within its own flow of cultural consciousness. It is an age in which we really no longer have grounds, it seems, even to condemn the Holocaust. In consequence our political leaders have already discarded the absoluteness of 'Never again' and are instead permitting it to be enacted anew.

By politics I mean the total range of public concerns, from the village to the universe, every activity or concern which is not primarily a matter of personal or family gain. Our own pursuits of food and drink, sex, learning, money, relaxation, our own personal spiritual lives, our fads and hobbies are not politics. Politics signifies all that relates beyond these to the common good of the human city. It takes up into itself even the professedly 'charitable', personal as that may be. If one buys an opera ticket, that is not a political act if one does it in order to enjoy the singing, but if one does it in order to support the opera company as part of the web of civic living then it becomes political. Trevor Huddleston's long campaign against apartheid is inherently political, wholly a priest as he is, but so too is Mother Teresa's campaign to provide shelter and dignity in dying for the poorest of the poor.

There can, of course, be no sharp line between the private and the political: so much depends on the motivation behind behaviour. In reality much of what is ostensibly highly publicly-orientated and political is the pursuit of private and group interest. Once uncovered, this is recognised as corruption. Because politics at its most explicit is inevitably about power, and public power is an easy lever for the private accumulation of wealth, it is of all areas of human activity the most prone to corruption. If we cannot afford to leave the politics of government to politicians, it is because the politician is always in it at least in part for personal gain; it is his or her private career and, despite appearances, the professional politician is often the least political of people in the true sense of the word. He is professionally assisted to turn what by its nature is the pursuit of the common good into a short cut to private gain and private power.

So widespread is, in such terms, the corruption of political life that you may think it purely utopian to define politics in the terms I suggest. Yet it is no more futile to cling doggedly to a classical conception of politics than to understand marriage or any other aspect of human existence in terms not only of the inescapable subjectivity of participants but also in terms of an objectivity of morality, meaning and purpose, a harmony of rationally-grounded relationships.

Almost everywhere such objectivities have in the past been defined, especially by the religious, in too simplistic, too unbending terms. Recognition of the relativities of culture and context must not however make us wholly abandon a sense of the objective. Pope John Paul is far more right in insisting on the reality of what we call 'Truth' and the splendour of it than he is wrong in the rigid and inadequate terms in which Rome remains set upon wanting to delimit it. To recognise that the law of the jungle, a plethora of subjectivities, of consciences, is part of reality is one thing, to canonise it as the *ne plus ultra* is quite another.

The slave trade was still highly profitable at the start of the nineteenth century, and it was still defended resolutely in terms of refusing to buck the laws of the market. When parliament voted for its abolition, it damaged the economy quite considerably but it committed Britain to the principle that at least in some cases the laws of the market must be subordinated to deeper laws of humanity and morality. Moreover, whatever politicians actually do, they endeavour time and again, when challenged, to portray their policies in terms of the common-good principles I have portrayed. Even a Stalin, a Ceaucescu or a Karadzic will do so. The phoniest lip service has still its own significance.

Let us turn to prayer. By this I mean personal or group activity whereby we place ourselves in the presence of God, of ultimate and objective love, truth, justice, mercy in all its plenitude, final incomprehensibility, yet unlimited demand upon the human conscience. By it we offer ourselves in service to do that most mysterious of courses, the 'Will of God'; that course of behaviour which, within the complexities of our muddled lives, comes closest to love and truth, to generosity and forgiveness, all that is best even if also, as often, much of what is hardest. By it we beseech strengthening, the inner resourcefulness of goodness, the light that cuts through cliché and clap-trap, the sheer resolution to work on at overcoming all within us and all around us that is opposed to some whisper of God's kingdom. Prayer means recognition of the transcendent, not merely intellectually – though that is implied – but affectively in mind and heart, across periods of time, upon our lips, in a certain stillness within the centre of our consciousness; a recognition which others do not need to see but may well suspect; a recognition that relates us here and now to an order of being above, below, within, without, before, after; an order of being which we believe presents the key of meaning, value, moral obligation; an ultimacy about what matters for every scrap of being we ourselves possess.

The central assertions of Christianity in which it differs most markedly from other religions, philosophies and ideologies lie in the paradoxical character of Jesus Christ, the Word that became 'flesh', Son of the eternal Father but wholly present inside the history of time, whom when we see we see the Father. Through the Incarnation Christianity combines transcendence with an exceptional degree of immanence, yet this Word still writes nothing, this Lord still dies an outcast on a cross. Wordship and Lordship here need a very singular interpretation. Within the normal order of history there is no way to reverse the Crucifixion. There in a very real sense the story ends and if we are to meet this Lord and hear this Word, we have still to do so in the crucified, the poor of this world, our neighbour in most need.

While the Christian tradition does not, and cannot, reject the affirmation of God with the qualities of omnipotence, omniscience and suchlike, qualities laboriously set out in many a textbook of theodicy, it has at its best effectively got beyond such a theology, both by insistence upon the *via negativa*, an insistence that we simply do not know what such words mean when we apply them to God, but also by the evangelical insight that we have been given Christ in which to see God, and that the qualities of the historical Christ are strikingly different from the qualities of the God of traditional theism. Inevitable strain here has produced the long night battle within Christology between those who want some old-fashioned deification of a too human Jesus, insisting that he must perform at least a few unlikely miracles, walking upon water or – in the Apocrypha – far more extraordinary prodigies, and those who strive, even against the formal witness of the gospels, to retain Jesus as Jesus.

I don't think it is possible to deny that the Christian tradition has here as elsewhere always been intellectually at war with itself. Is God like Jesus or must Jesus be made to appear like God, that is to say like the God of an unreconstructed theism? We cannot here convincingly appeal to a pre-schismatic, a pre-heretical, age. We have to live with the tensions within the history of our own beliefs. What, however, the final image of Calvary should make clear to us is that within human history we must expect divine omnipotence to be manifest above all in weakness, in no other way than it was manifested in Christ. The relationship between God and history becomes not one between the omnipotent and the finite but between the crucified and the society that destroyed him. The Christian vocation is to love and serve God in a world where God can only be revealed in such terms.

Without prayer and its grounding in faith, in the sense I have described it, the human city and its politics remain irredeemable. Selfishness and the corruption of sectional interests are too strong. But without politics prayer becomes a selfish ego-trip, an escape from that burden of secular reality for which every one of us is inherently responsible. A way to God which is not a way back hour by hour to our neighbour on the streets of Sarajevo is the way to a God who does not deserve either to be worshipped or to exist. He deserves rather to be abolished like so many other gods of the human past – abolished because in their strange attributes they never did exist, though some glimmer in their images may still have witnessed to what does and must exist beyond us all.

Every time prayer is detached from the politics of the market place, leaving the marketeers free to proclaim society intrinsically non-moral and the mystics free to proclaim a God concerned with the spiritual only, the core element of the specifically Christian is lost. Public things are material things; things that are spiritual only are private things. A religion of pure spirituality is a privatised religion with a privatised God, and a privatised God cannot or should not exist. God is the God of everything or of nothing, but of everything seen through the image of the crucified. Without such a God and without the human prayer that makes us conscious of such a God there can be no absolute critique of evil government and corrupt politics, no tradition of prophecy.

Could it be the case that, objectively, there is nevertheless no God whatever, that every image of God without exception is entirely and only a projection of humankind, objectively self-contradictory, and that Christians should go along with this, as objective atheists, while still creating god and religion for themselves as a sort of therapeutic spiritual game in ways each judges appropriate? Such is the position of the 'Sea of Faith' school, disciples of Don Cupitt, adapting thereby post-modernism to religion. The denial of objectivity is, in a way, very attractive, a wonderful way out of every philosophical and theological problem, but I don't believe that it is in any way intellectually obligatory. I also don't believe that it can conceivably retain ground for prophecy. It forfeits for the world what Christianity can still best offer. It represents a sophisticated privatisation of religion, but, in denying objectivity, it renders religion toothless in the public forum. It can assert no prophetic judgement on the sins of the state because it lays claim to no objectivity, superior to the state and to us all, against which to judge them. It cannot denounce genocide as diabolical, any more than it can condemn a crocodile for snatching a woman washing clothes at the river bank.

We can only prophesy out of an objectivity of truth and of goodness. If love is absolutely preferable to hate, truth to lies, whatever an individual chooses to think or do, then there exists over and above us a moral order, unchangeable, objective, absolute. That, as Aquinas would say, is what we call God. By prayer, in silence and meditation, we can open mind and heart to the overwhelming importance of the good and true, and realise the petty criminality of preferring the criteria of ethnic, party or commercial advantage. Out of prayer comes prophecy. Moreover in

Christ we discover that the God who is truth and goodness is none other than our neighbour in need. Prayer leads us to politics while politics can only be saved from itself by the prophecy which has come out of prayer.

There is, I would hold, no other model for Christian living which ever has been justified or can conceivably be justified. That is not to make us all into political activists in a narrow sense, any more than it should make us all into monks. Christian living is essentially communal: it is the life of a community, the Body of Christ, in which there are many members. The pre-eminently prayerful is needed at one end of the spectrum no less than the most committed activist at the other. Certainly there is some special danger in being at either end of the spectrum but if someone claims 'I have no need of thee' or, even, 'My role makes sense without yours', then there is trouble. Any explicit break in the totality of the system involves meaninglessness upon either side. The monastery inherently points to authority, values, ultimacy far beyond the Caesars of this world, or even beyond the CAFODs and Oxfams, but it also necessarily and inevitably provides at least some beginning of a realm of justice and mercy around it, an essentially secular reality, first for its own members by the very keeping of the rule, then for those who take sanctuary within its walls, but also at least by example and inspiration for a much wider world beyond.

The kingdom of God is not realisable upon earth and if we saw it we might not recognise it. But we can recognise its absence and we have at least the advantage over some ages of not deceiving ourselves in thinking that it is here, or almost here. We should, nevertheless, feel committed by both nature and grace to working for the unrealisable and to refusing to allow that human society is simply immoral. It is to an endeavour, not an achievement, that we are bound. If this is not recognised, and acted upon, if the flag is not unfurled again and again, upon even the most hopeless of battlefields, then the world will indeed have become instead the kingdom of Mammon, of the devil and all his accomplices, of the genocide of the unwanted, the multiplication of wealth for the powerful, of a systematic order of lies involving the control of all the media to ensure collective amnesia in regard to every history of successful evil, while filling each corner of time with the provision of 'almost reality' to keep the masses satisfactorily somnolent.

Is no one else but the Christian committed to fighting such horrors? Of course they are. The vocation of the Christian is the vocation of humanity. Here, as elsewhere, grace perfects but does not destroy nature.

We have many allies, believers and unbelievers. Nevertheless, the intellectual crumbling of both the socialist and the old liberal traditions have left most unbelievers particularly unsure of the grounding of any strong message to society. Other religious traditions are at least as unsettled within the culture of modernity as the Christian. It would be foolish to overcount the ranks of one's allies. Only great clarity of mind, confidence in the validity of the message and a high degree of moral commitment will bring people to resist the juggernauts of oppression – unless they are bulldozing one's own backyard. There have never been many people with these qualities. Even the Christian community has, generation after generation, been largely so disarmed by sheer weakness of vision, the attractions of other-worldliness or the pursuit of this-worldly advantage of its members, that its evangelical and prophetic voice has seldom sounded forth, with vehemence and subtlety, a this-worldly message that rings sharp and clear because it is derived both from the enlightenment obtained in prayer and from the enlightenment gained through every rational and intuitive tool open to the enquiring secular mind.

'He who would do good to another must do it in Minute Particulars. General Good is the plea of the scoundrel, hypocrite, and flatterer.' Minute Particulars. Blake's insistence is very relevant to our theme. There is a particularism in prophecy, just as there is a particularism in the Incarnation. It is easy enough for bishops or anyone else to come out with unreserved condemnations of ethnic cleansing, but we are not called as Christians to make general statements: we are called to do good in minute particulars. The politics of prophecy, of the gospel, is a politics which starts with, and must remain preoccupied with, the reality of individuals, one's neighbours in need. It starts, then, at a very different point from ideological politics, yet it does not and cannot be limited to the one-to-one relationships which rightly provide its initial model, as in the judgement scene of Matthew 25. When we serve 'one of these least ones' – hungry, thirsty, naked, stranger, sick, in prison – then we are in fact washing the feet of God. 'You did it to me.' But if that obligation is to be fulfilled, it has often to go far beyond a one-to-one relationship. The campaign to abolish the slave trade demonstrated this once and for all and, by doing so, created a permanent paradigm.

Everyone is against genocide in general, just as everyone likes the parable of the Good Samaritan so long as it is only a story that does not require anything actually of us. One cannot practise the option for the poor in general. One can only say that now in the Europe of the 1990s, our own Europe, genocide has gone on and on, effectively unchallenged. Day by day the terrified people of Mostar and Maglaj have been sniped at and shelled, just as the people of Srebreniza and Gorazde and Sarajevo have been sniped at and shelled and Europe has stood by with all the equipment needed to end this torture within hours, and has refused to do so. Our governments and our newspapers are desperate to find other things on which to concentrate our minds, but for the European Christian of today there is nothing else within our own continent with an even remotely comparable claim upon our Christian conscience. A church which does effectively nothing when faced with Bosnia is a church which has walked the road to Jericho as priest and Levite. It is a church, sad to say, to which we, both Catholics and Anglicans, undoubtedly belong.

There are, of course, many other claims upon our consciences today besides Bosnia. It is wholly legitimate for each member of the Body to take hold of that specific task of this-worldly caring that he or she can most effectively cope with, and there is a profound continuity of spirit between authentic instances at every level of response to the human needs of the other. Nevertheless societies and churches are challenged publicly at a given time by one or another dominating need – dominant in intensity of suffering, in social significance, in accessibility.

In the objectivity of history there has never, since the days when I was a schoolboy at Douai, been anything happening in Europe comparable to what has been taking place since early 1992 in Bosnia. It is true that Europe cannot be the policeman of the world and that what we cannot do we have no moral obligation to do. But as regards Bosnia, we could quite easily intervene. We could have done so long ago. Indeed we have intervened in several massive and highly damaging ways, thus recognising our responsibility. We have endeavoured to control the negotiating process through Lords Carrington and Owen. We have insisted upon an arms embargo upon a legitimate government. We have compelled that government to sit down at the negotiating table with the leaders of a terrorist movement far more evil and violent than the IRA, while we have kept declaring that on principle we could never discuss with men of violence over Northern Ireland. We have in fact done everything we could to legitimise violence and its consequences in Bosnia while verbally condemning it; and our churches, tied in one way or another only too closely to the state, have sought the advice of the Foreign Office and as a result do nothing but mouth banalities.

You may think that all this is a long way away from the theme of being a Christian today; I can only say that I can see no other way that with integrity I could be a Christian. The truth of prayer is bound to wilt if protected from the furnace of the politics of prophecy. In my childhood that was true in regard to the fate of the Jews; then, for years, the central issue became racialism and apartheid. Today it is the fate of whole peoples, whether Indians on the Amazon or Muslims in Bosnia. Tomorrow it will take other forms. The urgency inescapable in being a Christian must always focus on the here and now, on minute particulars.

The Christian vocation is inescapably political, but its politicism is bound to degenerate into party expediency if it is not held on a tight rein by the experience of prayer and a theology of the kingdom which never expects too much of the world but is never prepared to settle except for too much. It recognises that the hierarchical church is at least as much part of the world in its fallenness as part of any kingdom of grace. It holds that a God whose proclaimed representatives lay down meticulous rules of moral conduct over sexual matters but fail to fling themselves in to protect the victims of outrage does not merit faith. Too often the church is the best argument for atheism.

If Christ and Yahweh are not to become a mere part of our cultural past like Thor and Woden, it will depend not on some new demonstration of the efficacy of the Five Ways, not on the irrational hysteria of charismatics and fundamentalists, not on government insistence that Christianity of a sort be taught in our schools, but rather on the manifestation in our lives, fuelled by prayer, of such justice, such mercy, such moral courage, such truth-telling as to make humanity, faced with the appalling consequences of the amoral atheism which now increasingly dominates our culture and our society, actually rediscover a belief in Christ to be indeed 'Good News'.

Lecture given in Douai Abbey Church,
6 October 1993

3

Theology and Contemporary Reality

I take it that theology has a public function. It is not simply a formulation of personal belief – personal as every theology must be. If, *pace* Lady Thatcher, society exists, humanity exists as a whole and corporately, then to function even moderately well it must do so on the grounding of some rationale. And, of course, it does, or tries to. Unfortunately that rationale is very wobbly at present and it is wobbly partly because of the decline of theology and particularly of a public theology.

For its part, if theology has no claim to speak to society it has, I believe, no claim to be considered something serious in its own right. It cannot survive simply as a guide for personal and private life, or as a study of past history, of texts, of religious phenomena. Its very claim to be about God has necessarily to be a claim about everything else, and particularly everything of great importance – not *de minimis* – though sometimes we give just the opposite impression. Theology has to be, if it is to be at all, an interpretation of the totality of reality in regard to its ultimate significance. And reality is contemporary. So far as we are concerned, any other reality can only come to us through that which is contemporary. In a secular age, the theologian has either to pack up shop or to stick his neck out. It may seem brash to lay claim to the high moral ground in regard to life as a whole; it may seem dangerous, but we really have no alternative.

Theology is a science. It cannot dismiss anything relevant known by other sciences, and it has moreover itself to proceed as rationally as it can. That does not mean avoiding the intuitive and the imaginative: a total rationality of understanding includes the poetic, the prophetic, whatever. Nor is it less a matter of faith, a leap of holistic interpretation that goes not against reason but beyond it, as every great intuition must do. Theology interprets all else that matters in the context of faith that God is, and in the light of that faith – God, the utterly unimaginable and yet that which most is. It is because there is something that is more ultimate than ourselves or than anything else, something we cannot alter, that we can interpret all else in its light. It is what we call God.

Does God matter? Does theology matter? If God is, then it must matter that he is. By definition. If he is not, then clearly he cannot matter. To ask the question usefully, we must rephrase it. Can we show that anything is different if we assert God than if we do not? Can the world be quite the same for you and me though you believe in God and I do not? In fact that is often the case either because the non-believer continues to function with the presuppositions of a society that did believe, or because the believer has adopted the culture and conviction of a society of unbelief, and merely clips onto them a personal affirmation of belief without consequences other than those of a very private nature.

Nevertheless I cannot believe that we can logically understand the human predicament and our responsibilities within it in the same way, with or without God. Our society is in reality now an atheist one. God and religion mean next to nothing in public terms. It is arguable that this truth has nothing to do with society's enormous disorientation, that it has been produced by a range of other causes or simply human inability to cope with the social consequences of the ongoing technological revolution.

What is certain is that there does exist a huge ideological vacuum in our world, an ever-worsening and widening social and political crisis and an almost complete absence of any significant public affirmation of religion. A claim for the hegemony of theology in such circumstances is surely worth making, so long as it can be made convincingly. If others can put forward good claims for alternative hegemonic doctrines let them do so by all means, but one does not see many around.

There is in fact a dominant hegemony in our society: it is the hegemony of Mammon, of the market, but a market controlled by the very rich, twisted to ensure that their power and wealth is protected. Theology – or anything else which is to challenge that – has both to see its brutal, unglitzy reality and to be able to put forward an alternative. Anything laying claim to hegemony must be able to offer a coherent public doctrine, of both being and doing; a doctrine that can lay claims upon us, and upon society as a whole, not only a select group of believers, that can provide convincing imperatives which actually challenge us to think, and to behave, differently from the way people do without it.

I believe that theology can in principle still do this today, that it is by its nature bound to do so, though by and large it is not doing so. I believe too that our human situation desperately needs it to be done, but that it is only possible if theology re-emerges from preoccupation with individual salvation and that preoccupation's latest post-modernist expression, the pick and choose culture of the Sea of Faith school. Is genocide wrong? Is the construction of a society in which more and more people are being left permanently unemployed wrong? Are these and other things so wrong that we should be gripped to struggle against them? If so – why? I do not see any reason to say they are very wrong in the terms of the current public doctrine of Mr Major's society. I do not see any convincing theoretical reason and I do not see that they in fact matter very much to those who increasingly control our society. I cannot myself see any secular grounding for an absolute, unequivocal judgement of right and wrong, anything sufficient to undergird with intrinsic authority the voice of prophecy.

It is perfectly true that in ages when Christianity was accepted as the public doctrine of our society, some pretty fearful evils were defended by both political leaders and church leaders. That was partly because Christianity itself was formulated and understood in ways that actually encouraged, even demanded, some of those evils. Nevertheless, there did still exist a hegemonic doctrine from which many crimes could be assessed and condemned. Today there is none. The decline of three things – Christianity, the assured liberal humanism which had grown up on largely Protestant foundations, and the many branched tree of socialism – have left us with a hegemonic vacuum. That gap needs filling but if Christian theology wishes to fill it – and I hardly see the point of theology existing at all, unless it believes itself capable of such a role – then it has to be clear what it is trying to do. It has to have a message which actually matters to the central issues of society, which is believable and believed in, which recognises its limitations while playing to its strengths, which has an adequate internal coherence while not attempting to smooth out every problem. It requires to be complex, subtle, and sufficiently grounded in contemporary reality to meet the intellectual and public needs of human beings convincingly though not infallibly. It is a lot to ask.

There are periods in human history when the organised city of man has appeared to be endeavouring to seek very much what the City of God is seeking. There develops a sort of alliance – sometimes a dangerous and deceptive alliance – between them. In our own century that was, I believe, the case from the 1940s to the 1970s. The age of the United Nations, of the winding up of empire, of the blossoming of the Commonwealth, of the welfare state and the National Health Service, the ending of capital punishment, was, at least for this country, an age in which the church could have little of a prophetic voice because it could only confirm what society and the state were endeavouring to do. Within that wide context, however, there could still be a need for outspokenness and contestation over specific issues, as Archbishop Michael Ramsey showed on several matters.

Perhaps there is a self-complacent quality in such periods; anyway, they do not last. Today we are certainly in a different situation. It is quite impossible to bless or be content with the way society is going or the values underlying it, although one sees rather little evidence that church leadership has become aware of the extent of the challenge. On the whole ecclesiastical and ecumenical leadership appears, on the contrary, to be withdrawing from any sustained assessment or challenging of the public domain into far more specifically religious and evangelical preoccupations. If church leadership were to try to meet this challenge it would certainly require a very considerable theological contribution, but compared with a generation ago what strikes one is a decline in the level of academic contribution for which church leaders now look.

It may help us at this point if we cast our minds back about sixty years, to the 1930s, a decade to whose atmosphere we are getting uncomfortably close. The alliance which dominated the next forty years had not begun to exist. That very absence may help us find in the 1930s resources which we need today. It was a time when under huge social and political pressure church leaders were attempting to re-articulate a public doctrine able to cope with Fascism, Nazism, Communism and unemployment. We see it in the Oxford Conference of 1937 on 'Church, Community and State', in the ongoing contribution of William Temple and George Bell, in the books of Christopher Dawson, R. H. Tawney and Jacques Maritain, in the social thinking of the Student Christian Movement and the beginnings of the World Council, even in the development of Catholic social teaching through the encyclical *Quadragesimo Anno* (a development which would only approach maturity twenty-five years later in the Vatican Council in the 1960s and the encyclicals of Pope John and Pope Paul).

Despite diversities, I don't think it unreasonable to suggest that there was a large degree of coherence in all this and that despite weaknesses – some of which would be made good with the emergence of Liberation Theology – it offered a public doctrine able to unite Catholics, Anglicans, Presbyterians and others. Grounded both on natural law and morality as an inbuilt expression of the divine will in humankind and a more evangelical call to pursue a kingdom of God upon earth, it could at least attempt to wrestle with the greatest issues of the day at once with intellectual analysis, statesmanlike diplomacy and a prophetic voice. It was the great age of ecumenism, but it was not inhibited by the Ecumenical Movement from being politically serious in a way that has, unfortunately, come subsequently to be the case.

All this may sound over-sanguine for it is equally true that the churchmen and theologians of the 1930s too often failed to agree, too often held back in caution from committing themselves to even the gravest of causes, while some of their more excitable camp-followers rushed headlong into highly simplistic commitments, particularly pacifist ones. The fact is that the kind of public doctrine I am suggesting only just existed and was quite inadequately appropriated. Headlam, Bishop of Gloucester, and formerly Regius Professor of Divinity at Oxford, the academic heavyweight on the bench of bishops, was a boring theologian and a disastrous political guide. Henson of Durham was superb on Abyssinia but had been appalling on the General Strike. Even Bell of Chichester, by far the most clear-sighted of prophetic ecclesiastics, by no means always got it right, while Temple, the quintessential leader of churchmen, was at heart too much of an English establishmentarian, too temperamentally averse to adopting an unpopular position, too unable to grasp the sheer wickedness of a world whose progressing goodness he had most of his life seen no reason to question. Dawson retreated to his study, Maritain retreated to Canada. Perhaps only Bell actually grew in stature, in clarity of mind and in sheer moral power, as the situation got worse. And he did it by refusing to steer clear of the particular. When he attacked the saturation bombing of German towns and was accused by government spokesmen of betraying the British airmen who risked their lives in such exercises (and many lost them), he refused to be silenced by that ancient ploy of policy-makers who try to ensure that bad policies are protected from criticism by being hidden behind the courage of those who carry them out.

Bell, Karl Barth once declared, was still too much of an English gentleman to understand Hitler. It remains dangerous to be a gentleman, to cultivate a certain niceness in oneself which makes one sure that everyone else must be nice too. Without a very strong sense of the power of sin, of evil in the world, it is impossible to formulate a theology of politics or of history, or to defend the ground out of which effective prophecy can come. Turn from Bell to Gerhard Kittel, that very distinguished German New Testament scholar, creator of the great *Wörterbuch* but also author of an appalling theological apologia for the Nazi race laws, *Die Judenfrage*. When Kittel was invited to lecture on the New Testament in Cambridge in 1937, he wore his Nazi badge. Has the theological community ever seriously interrogated itself upon why it was able to hold within it not only Kittel but many other Nazi sympathisers? What use was theology to Germany in the 1930s?

An answer may be offered in Barth and Bonhoeffer. We can fairly compare Kittel with Bonhoeffer, though Kittel had a recognised academic position while Bonhoeffer had not. Neither was representative. Each had to wrestle with a fairly intractable theological legacy to get where he did. Theology, like the churches in their central leadership, has been far better at providing a public doctrine to confirm the state than to challenge it, and that was especially true of the Lutheran tradition.

In practice theologians have mostly had too narrow an ecclesiastical and biblical culture to be able to relate their work effectively to the needs of contemporary secularity. Nor, of course, has the kind of theology they have held generally urged such a relationship. While Temple was looking for ways to extend the relationship, his concept of the 'middle axiom' tended in practice to cut the relationship short before it could be effective. It may only be with Liberation Theology that a group of theologians have accepted the responsibility to try to carry the message right through to the particularities of the present. It is theologically correct that a religion which starts with the particularity of the Incarnation and is, in Temple's phrase, 'the most materialistic of religions', should in its theology reach back to the particular. It has, of course, always done so, indeed excessively, in regard to the sexual and the marital. It is actually more appropriate that it should do so in regard to social and political justice.

It is perfectly open to argument that Liberation Theology has in some of its expressions taken on board unhelpful Marxist luggage. Once one accepts the obligation to speak a contemporary language, such things are inevitable. Nevertheless the central thrust of Liberation Theology does little more than re-articulate in an emphatic way the central thrust of Christian concern down the ages with justice, peace and the primacy of the poor. It theologises what was always there. Can it however actually make theology useful? One may well have the feeling that it is not theology but prophecy which can be shown to relate effectively, in so far as anything does, to contemporary public need, and that Bell and Bonhoeffer remain better exemplars of prophecy than they are of theology. As a matter of fact and the European theological tradition, that may be true. The question is rather whether theology can justify and provide the ground for such prophecy; whether it mentally shapes a church and its bishops to hearken to prophecy, whether it suggests connections and leaves its hearers on their toes to look for more; or whether, on the contrary, it encourages its addicts to concentrate their attention on churchy and scriptural realities perceived as alternative to the world of politics, poverty and oppression, instead of as keys to the conversion of that world.

While theology is by no means identical with prophecy, it should judge its effectiveness precisely as theology, not in terms of the purely academic production of a Wörterbuch, but in the extent to which it has provided a public doctrine usable by prophets, who can combine an evangelical eye with both passion and a subtle sanity.

The complexity of the troubles we are faced with now is well beyond anything our society has had to cope with since the 1930s, both in the seriousness of the social disfunctioning and the intellectual and moral confusion as to how to respond. The Thatcherism of ten years ago, with its quality of an anti-socialist crusade for the recovery of freedom, was something in which its leader at least believed. It did have a certain moral note about it, but that surely has gone. It has been replaced by something which might better be called wealthism. No one in their senses could believe that the interests of the population of this country as a whole are served by the privatisation of the railways: that does not matter. Any privatisation will add further to the pool of large-scale property which can be manipulated to increase both the wealth of the very wealthy and the power of the very wealthy, a new superclass of which our political rulers quickly become members. Everything moreover is being done to reduce the multiplicity of independent powers within our society. Local government, the universities, the trade unions have all lost enormously in power over the last years, as have the churches. What is replacing them is the centralised state and the plutocracy, the two held together by an interlocking of interest and of personnel.

Surprising as it may seem, I believe that the advance of post-modernism is comparable in the intellectual world with that of neo-Thatcherism in the socio-political. Each is eroding the structures, the order, the frontiers, the diversity of authorities, that are required for civil society and for the civilisation of the mind. If increasingly our society is bereft of the ability even to criticise what is being done to it, then it is because potential critics have been disarmed by the very nature of contemporary cultivated discourse. In my view, the post-Cupitt 'Sea of Faith' tendency is doing to theology and to belief what post-modernism is doing to intellectual culture as a whole and neo-Thatcherism to our society. All are removing objectivity, what Cupitt calls 'realism', replacing recognition of the absolute with the satisfaction of 'customers': develop your own religion, one is told, rather in the way Mrs Thatcher declared that she was increasing freedom of choice, or Murdoch offers the freedom of scores of separate television channels. There is a kind of consumerist freedom which provides the high road to slavery.

It is from within such a home culture that we look beyond Britain to genocide in Bosnia, to the arising of Fascist nationalisms in many other countries, to the economic and political collapse of much of the third world – and with it the steady decline in the aid we give it – and to the central collapse of the United Nations as a serious, effective and moral agency for the pursuit of international justice. Wealthism, nationalism, racism are all undergirded both by the collapse of a shared intellectual community of moral absolutes, out of which it was possible to condemn the Holocaust in a way that carried with it genuine contemporary authority, and by the development of systematic deception by both government and big business of a sort that we have seen in the 'arms for Iraq' case, the running of the Maxwell empire and in numerous other instances.

The burden of church responsibility for the world, of Christian and human responsibility, has to be to stand up to all these forces for the sake of a community of justice, peace and equality. This can only be done if there is a sustained intellectual and strategic exercise far beyond anything we have seen for years – well beyond, for instance, the quite limited, though real, 1980s achievement of *Faith in the City*. I see very little sign that church leaders or theologians have begun to realise the scale of their responsibility. If they should realise it, they certainly could not begin to shoulder it without a formidable range of qualities and skills.

The first is a shared theology: a theology both of God and of the world, a theology of the absoluteness, the decisiveness and the meaningfulness of truth, love, justice and peace and the necessity of their pursuit here and now. You may call that Liberation Theology. You can as well call it the central strand of a healthy Christian consciousness across all the ages.

The second is an acquired skill in understanding the secular, not being frightened of it, not being bullied by the powers that be into adopting their ways of seeing things, not above all claiming that as religious leaders or theologians it is not our task actually to grapple with the secular. One has to, even though one will make mistakes. The only alternative is to be silly. I am afraid clerical silliness is very common, and very often establishmentarian. One can see it, for instance, in the report of the commission of British churchmen which visited ex-Yugoslavia early in 1993, went to Belgrade and Zagreb, talked about the long-standing religious tensions between Orthodox Serbs and Catholic Croats, but managed – when war and genocide were raging in Bosnia – to say almost nothing about what was by far the most important thing going on in ex-Yugoslavia. It avoided any serious reference to Muslims. Why? I can see two main reasons. One, to say anything significant or true about Bosnia must mean taking sides in a way that would look unecumenical, particularly for Anglicans, over-anxious not to offend the Orthodox; the other that the Foreign Office did not want it, and the delegation was only too clearly dependent upon the Foreign Office from first to last. A modest erastian establishment seemed almost tolerable in the age of Macmillan, Wilson or Heath. In the age of Major and the moral decline of Whitehall which goes with it, any degree of erastianism whatsoever is becoming quite intolerable. If being an established church means being ingratiatingly dependent upon the mind and intentions of such a state, the Foreign Office of Mr Hurd, the Home Office of Mr Howard, then it is as much the devil here as being a 'German Christian' in Hitler's Reich or a conformist Orthodox in the Soviet Union of Stalin or Brezhnev.

Besides a living theology, a skill in analysing the secular and freedom from erastianism, there is required the harnessing of a strong will. Again and again we say, correctly I believe, that where the government fails over this or that matter is not in the means but in lack of political will. What it wants to do, it does, foolish as it may be, like the community charge or the privatisation of the railways. When it says it can't do something, such as stop genocide in Bosnia, it is not in fact because it cannot but because it lacks any will to do so. But a lack of real effective will affects other people too. With each of us, singly, and with every group of church people or theologians or whatever, the question has to be asked. What really do we want? How much does child abuse or racial persecution or mass unemployment or the destruction of the rain forests or the repetition of the Holocaust actually matter to us? How many hours, how many pounds will we give that this should not be? Only collective action can be effective: how far are we willing, not just to have opinions, but to work together with others? Nothing is easy. What is certain is that nothing is possible without the will to make it so, and that many things which seem impossible until they are emphatically willed by a group of committed people then become possible.

Professional theologians cannot be a substitute for bishops or ordinary people or prophets, or, indeed, for a far wider group of the theologically aware. One can but be a trigger to develop a sense of vision, to get a movement started. One can but say: Look on this picture and on this. Look on Jesus Christ, or Francis of Assisi, the anti-slavery campaigners, or George Bell and Dietrich Bonhoeffer. And now look on the world around you. Is that tradition represented here? Is it not needed? Has society ever been more explicitly dominated by Mammon than now? Would it not benefit from the recovery of a public doctrine at once appropriate to our own age and in line with that which as human beings we identify with and have adhered to in the past?

A public doctrine combines the spiritual, the moral, the political, the social. It requires theology but also a great deal more than theology, but without it there is nothing to withstand the heartless march towards a world ruled by Mammon, in which justice and mercy are ruled out as unaffordable. If theology has a contemporary task to perform, it is beyond all else to defend the foundations of a public doctrine according to which it is possible to judge and to prevent the excesses of the heartlessness of the powerful.

A lecture given at the West Midlands Ministerial Training Course,
Birmingham
9 November 1993

The Context
for Prophecy

4

The University and the World
The Paradox of Newman's 'Idea'

Newman's *Idea of a University* seems surrounded by paradox. It is perfectly true, and entirely clear from the book itself, that Newman was a person deeply concerned with the functioning of a university. He was not merely a great thinker and writer, he was also deep in his being a university man. His battles in Oxford had not only been to Catholicise the Church of England, they had also been – and had originally been – a struggle to reinvigorate university teaching. As a tutor at Oriel he had been a Young Turk, preoccupied with the reform of academic methodology. Yet the fact remains that he attained in Oxford no university position or professorship – unlike Pusey or even Keble – and his most memorable impact was achieved from the pulpit of St Mary's. His was felt above all as a religious impact, then and afterwards. Ten years later he jumped at the invitation to guide the proposed new Catholic university in Dublin and, even before being appointed to that post officially, he wrote and delivered his discourses upon the nature of a university. Moreover, during his years as Rector he adopted a very realistic and rather modern stance in the extremely uphill task of creating a university in a distinctly unfavourable terrain.

I find it particularly moving to read his *Address to the Evening Classes* or his *Address to the Medical Students*. These were his last university addresses and I do not believe one will find many mid-nineteenth-century vice-chancellors addressing either the one or the other. Yet, to return to the apparent paradox, we do not usually think of Newman in regard to such, quite secular, concerns. The whole Dublin episode can easily be made to appear as but an aberration in his life and, in a way, it was. He might after all have made a success of the university, despite all the awkwardness of the Irish bishops, if he had been prepared to give it his whole mind; but he was not. Rightly or wrongly, within what he himself called 'my double allegiance',[1] the Birmingham Oratory did come first. It is not reasonable to blame Cardinal Cullen for the whole misadventure. It expressed as much the inner tension within Newman himself: a great nineteenth-century educational pioneer struggling inside a great and intensely spiritual, even other-worldly, religious genius.

The paradox is reflected in the inability of his contemporaries to take note of *The Idea*. When the *Apologia* was published ten years later, they applauded. The *Apologia* fitted with the image of Newman his own world had of him. It mellowed that image undoubtedly, but it was congruent with the way the world saw him. *The Idea* was not and it was almost wholly ignored. Curiously, it is still – I would judge – somewhat under-used by the main body of Newman specialists. They are, on the whole, theologians and this is the least theological of all his main works. And yet this book, which could almost not exist and the main lines of the generally accepted portrait of Newman would remain, I venture to suggest, virtually untouched, is of all his works now the most widely read and referred to. It is undoubtedly the most prophetic.

The most profoundly religious of all eminent Victorians was yet able here to delineate the fundamental character of the greatest and most intrinsically secular of institutions with a sureness as to its overall nature, an accuracy of detailed analysis, and above all a sensitive sympathy which can make one gasp and ask at points in the argument: Which side is he really on? The paradox goes very deep. It derives not just from an occupational incompatibility between Newman the Birmingham Oratorian and Newman the Dublin Vice-Chancellor, or even between an anti-modernist theologian and the pragmatic requirements of a mid-nineteenth-century educational institution. It derives rather from an intrinsic abiding tension within all his work – a tension which comes to the surface again and again in many contexts, but never more clearly than in *The Idea of a University*. Owen Chadwick has remarked of this book, 'There is no sense of tension. This is one of the elements in the *Idea* which makes it unique'.[2] I find this an extraordinary judgement and am quite sure that nothing is less true. *The Idea* appears to me unintelligible except within a context of tension, both external and internal to Newman; but when we have understood that tension we may actually find it enlightening for the interpretation not only of his problems but also of ours.

The Idea was written in the 1850s. It was a time when university expansion and reform were very much under way both in Britain and elsewhere. Newman's Oxford itself, which he had left seven years before, was about to be reformed. In England the ancient monopoly of Oxford and Cambridge had been challenged by University College, London, with its stridently secularist stance; and University College had itself been challenged, in a way, by the foundation of King's College, London, and by Durham. The relationship of university and church was at the heart of nearly all these developments. In the north of England Manchester and other future civic universities were just beginning to emerge. In Ireland the Queen's Colleges had been begun by Peel in an attempt to cater for Catholics in a non-denominational way, thus bypassing Trinity College, still as Anglican as Oxford or Cambridge.

Not only in Ireland were Catholic university needs increasingly being felt. On the continent of Europe Louvain had been refounded. In the United States, where universities of all sorts were multiplying rapidly, Notre Dame in Indiana was founded in 1844. In this movement of expansion, two lines of advance matter to us here. One was away from the ecclesiastical, the denominational, the theological, towards the open, the non-discriminating and the scientific. University College, London, is here the model of modernisation, but it represents a general direction: the pursuit of the educationally efficient, the utilitarian, within a pluralist society. Newman did not care for it temperamentally, seeing it fairly enough as part of the process of secularist liberalisation which was removing religion to the non-intellectual margin of life. Behind it lay a philosophy he saw himself as battling against lifelong. Yet the fierce opposition he felt for it as a young Tory cleric in the Oxford of the 1830s had in practice largely disappeared in the really more open-minded Catholic priest of the 1850s.

The second line of advance was the endeavour to universitise Catholics, who in Britain since the Reformation and more widely since the Revolution had been largely left out of higher education. The need for Catholic graduates was becoming clear. It had been quite obvious to Newman from within a month of his conversion in 1845; indeed he appears almost immediately to have seen his Catholic vocation as lying, not in the conversion of other non-Catholics to Catholicism (which is what most Catholics expected of him) but instead in the conversion of Catholics themselves both to the educational standards he had taken for granted as an Anglican and to a theology which did justice to history.

But Newman was a great realist, someone living far more in the present day – however much he often disliked the present day – than either admirers or critics may imagine. Hence, while he disliked the ideals of Bentham or Brougham exceedingly, he actually took on board far more of their utilitarian educational practice than might seem conceivable for the former tutor of Oriel. When suddenly in 1851 the proposal came from Archbishop Cullen that he should head a university in Ireland, he could not but warm to the opportunity. Here surely was the challenge he was inwardly awaiting: to shape a Catholic university – as he saw it for the whole of the British Empire, or the English-speaking world, not just Ireland – which would embody the collegial experience of Oxford, the orderly government of Louvain and all that was pragmatically acceptable in the latest pioneering developments of the new universities.

His theoretical model remained, curiously enough, a medieval university with its four faculties and four nations: Newman's university in theory takes off from just the point reached, shall we say, by Bishop Elphinstone's Aberdeen in the early 1500s, however different it would be in practice. Later, in 1863, Newman was to remark, 'From first to last, education ... has been my line'.[3] So Cullen's invitation simply brought to the surface what had long been fundamental to his purposes, hidden though it may largely have been to the observer. Yet from the start he recognised how difficult it would be to do justice to both the movements I have outlined – to be both secularising and Catholicising – and in such a way as could satisfy not only him but also the Irish bishops.

The nine discourses constituting the first part of *The Idea* and written before he began his work as Rector were produced at Cullen's specific request to give 'a few lectures on education' to set the ball rolling. What Cullen wanted of these lectures was 'to persuade the people that education should be religious',[4] the underlying justification in fact for rejecting the Queen's Colleges and attempting to establish a specifically Catholic university. Here began the problem. Newman did, of course, wholly accept Cullen's basic rationale. He had longed for a Catholic English-language university since becoming a Catholic, he disliked secularist education, he certainly wanted theology to be within a university. The whole point of his coming to Dublin was that Cullen and others among the bishops – though not Murray of Dublin – were against a non-religious university such as Peel had offered them, and in principle Newman agreed.

Yet he only agreed up to a point, for the more deeply he had pondered the intrinsic nature of a university, the more he had divined the difficulty in imposing upon it a too religious form. The public agenda of the discourses was to argue the case for a religious university. The hidden agenda was rather to convince the bishops and anyone else in Dublin who would listen that, while they would indeed be getting a Catholic university, it would still have to be a university and it is of the nature of a university to be itself, something profoundly free, the embodiment of a truly liberal education, almost – one might say – a necessarily secular institution.

It is as an exercise in strategy that *The Idea* should first be examined. How was the Oxford Englishman, the recent convert with all the cultural appearance of a Protestant clergyman, going to persuade Catholic Irishmen with little or no academic experience to back the sort of thing Newman believed a university must be? The heavy stress upon the importance of theology in the first four discourses must surely be interpreted largely as a strategic necessity. It vindicated Cullen. It provided an apparent rationale for not going along with the Queen's Colleges. It demonstrated Newman's religious and Catholic commitment. But it did little more. As he wrote most revealingly to Robert Ornsby in April 1852 the subject of his first lectures 'will seem *dry* but (in confidence) they were suggested by high authority, and I think may please those whom I most wish to please, if I begin with them ... After these I shall go on to give a normal idea of a university'.[5]

Needless to say, Newman did sincerely believe theology to be important, indeed essential, for a true university, but he was far from thinking it the centre of a university and if he spends the first hundred pages of *The Idea* defending its presence, this had much less to do with his Idea and far more with the necessity of conciliating Rome, Cullen and the Irish church generally. But it does contribute to the paradox of the book, though the paradox is only superficially one relating to the immediate circumstances of its production, while far more deeply being one relating to the unending struggle within Newman's mind between dogma and modernism. It is, one might claim, the only one of his books in which, in a certain way, it is actually the latter which controls the argument and enjoys the more endearing warmth of expression.

Newman, did, of course, have his heart in the argument that theology has a most necessary place in a university. It was not only to please Cullen and guarantee his orthodox credentials that he started this way and spent so much time upon it. When jousting against University College, London, and a wider secularising tendency, he was nevertheless digging up rather dated material from twenty years earlier in his life and he seems now little perturbed by the tendency he criticises. He rightly points out how the foundation of University College had been countered by that of King's – a sense of the to-and-fro of things, the way an excess in one direction is rectified in the course of time by a counter-thrust in another, being very much part of his perennial thought; and it has proved the case.

Thus, when the new civic universities in the midlands and north of England developed in the second half of the nineteenth century, they all initially and fairly deliberately excluded theology – though only Liverpool actually wrote that exclusion into its constitution. In due course, nevertheless, they all have – with the sole exception of Liverpool – introduced theology into their programmes, and even Liverpool has altered its constitution to make this possible. That would have pleased Newman, and especially that in his own Birmingham a flourishing department of theology should have developed. But he would not have been surprised; it is the way he expects history to go.

It must be stressed that, despite the space accorded in the discourses to the case for theology, he does not in fact argue that case in special terms but only as one discipline among many, none of which should be in principle excluded, for 'knowledge is a whole' and it is 'the very profession of a university to teach all sciences', so one must not of deliberation exclude even one. If theology is 'a real science occupied upon Truth' it has a right to be present but really only as good a claim as any other. If theology be excluded, its province, he argues rather prophetically, 'will actually be usurped by other sciences' (I. IV.15). Its subject-matter, in fact, is unavoidable, but it is there, all the same, simply as one 'constituent portion' of what Newman calls Philosophy (I.IX.1).

If a concern for theology yet remains tangential to the central point of his book, it is worth noting that Newman does put his finger acutely enough on the problem of theology in most modern universities, especially Catholic ones. Effectively it had, and often does, become a form of professional training rather than the pursuit of knowledge for its own sake. Now Newman is insistent that professional education, even if it be theology (I.V.4), is extremely secondary to the purpose of a university, however valuable it may be in itself. As the Catholic bishops of his time would almost certainly fear, far more than want, a theology which went much beyond professional clerical training, this left very little room in practice for theology in Newman's university. It is perhaps not surprising, then, that it appears as the least of his concerns as Rector. He is much more preoccupied to get medicine or engineering off the ground.

He certainly did feel the need for General Religious Knowledge as part of the programme of the School of Arts, but that he saw as something rather different from theology. 'Religion', in the context of the 'School of Philosophy and Letters', he was convinced could best be studied historically 'simply as a branch of knowledge' (II. IV. 4) – rather more like Religious Studies as it has come to be known a century later. Of course Newman did personally want a theology which would go beyond the historical, literary and phenomenological study of religion, just as it would go beyond professional clerical training. But he was realistic enough to see that there was little immediate practical scope for this. And the problem still remains, theological teaching in universities being mostly orientated either towards professional training or towards a Religious Studies methodology. That may well be wise. It is certainly often inevitable.

Despite the first four discourses of *The Idea*, with their strongly apologetic note, theology in Newman's university was present then little more than in Newman's mind; but as it was a great mind, a great theological mind, and as it was precisely a theological mind that gave us *The Idea of a University*, let us – before leaving this topic only tangential to *The Idea* – listen for a moment to one of his most precise and disarming accounts of the relationship between theology and the other sciences. The confident Christian believer, he declares

> knows full well there is no science whatever, but, in the course of its extension, runs the risk of infringing, without any meaning of offence on its own part, the path of other sciences: and he knows also that, if there be any one science which, from its sovereign and unassailable position can calmly bear such unintentional collisions on the part of the children of earth, it is Theology. He is sure, and nothing shall make him doubt, that, if anything seems to be proved by astronomer or geologist, or chronologist, or antiquarian, or ethnologist, in contradiction to the dogmas of faith, that point will

eventually turn out, first, *not* to be proved, or secondly, not *contradictory*, or thirdly, not contradictory to any thing *really revealed*, but to something which has been confused with revelation. And if, at the moment, it appears to be contradictory, then he is content to wait, knowing that error is like other delinquents; give it rope enough, and it will be found to have a strong suicidal propensity. I do not mean to say that he will not take his part in encouraging, in helping forward the prospective suicide; he will not only give the error rope enough, but show it how to handle and adjust the rope; – he will commit the matter to reason, reflection, sober judgment, common sense; to Time, the great interpreter of so many secrets ... He will recollect that, in the order of Providence, our seeming dangers are often our greatest gains; that in the words of the Protestant poet,

> The clouds you so much dread
> Are big with mercy, and shall break
> In blessings on your head. (II. IV. 4)

That was the kind of thing both churchmen and scientists rather needed to hear said in a relaxed tone in the middle of the nineteenth century.

It is, however, not in the lectures on theology but in the later discourses that we find the central argument of *The Idea*: Newman's account of what he had privately described as the 'normal idea of a University'. The historical core of the European university, he correctly claimed, had always consisted, not in the faculties of Theology, Medicine or Law but in that of Arts. From the beginning of it all in the early thirteenth century until today the quintessential university man is the MA – whether it be in Oxford or Glasgow. Arts meant for Newman the study of knowledge as a whole in all its parts. At times he argues for Classics as providing its best methodology, but it is 'Philosophy' that he calls it again and again. All other sciences he sees, in a sense, as being part of 'Philosophy'. 'They are all quarried out of one and the same great subject of man's moral, social and feeling nature', he declares, quoting from his old Oriel colleague, John Davidson (I. IV. 9).

Newman did not wish in any way to exclude from a university's concern the physical sciences. On the contrary, and he was in this a self-conscious Aristotelian, it is the totality of concern with knowledge as such, all knowledge, which provides a university's distinctive character.

The grandeur of such a role makes him almost lyrical. It is, he declares in an 1855 lecture on Scientific Investigation:

> the high protecting power of all knowledge and science, of fact and principle, of inquiry and discovery, of experiment and speculation; it maps out the territory of the intellect, and sees that the boundaries of each province are religiously respected, and that there is neither encroachment nor surrender on any side. It acts as umpire between truth and truth, and, taking into account the nature and importance of each, assigns to all their due order of precedence. It maintains no one department of thought exclusively, however ample and noble; and it sacrifices none. It is deferential and loyal, according to their respective weight, to the claims of literature, of physical research, of history, of metaphysics, of theological science. It is impartial towards them all, and promotes each in its own place and for its own object. (II. VIII. 2)

What a claim! One might think that such a passage, composed by a Roman Catholic theologian and claiming for an institution that it 'acts as umpire between truth and truth', must be speaking of the Catholic Church. But no, Newman is speaking of the university. He does indeed feel himself bound at this point to reserve the higher rights of the church, perhaps a little uncomfortably, as sovereign in the order of grace to which nature must pay homage, as reason to revelation. Nevertheless, in the order of nature, and in regard to the immediate end and purpose of a university, he takes nothing back. He does, on the contrary, much stress the internal autonomy of the natural order, the ultimate harmony of nature and grace, but also the existential inevitability of a great deal of tension between institutions representative of the two. What is striking is his determination, in the later discourses especially, not to sell the university short in its necessary secularity, despite his own overwhelming personal commitment to Christian faith, religion and dogma.

It is in the last five discourses that Newman develops most fully the idea of a university whose proper scope is 'a Knowledge which is its own end ... liberal knowledge', not primarily knowledge as a matter of research but as something to be shared formatively between teachers and students. Newman's university is neither a research institution nor a school of professional training – it is a community of scholars and students pursuing the totality of truth, through a range of disciplines, simply because that is the best thing in the world for human beings to do. A recognition that knowledge, 'philosophy' in the large sense in which he uses it, intellectual culture, is absolutely worth pursuing for its own sake, regardless of useful mechanical inventions or professional training is, for Newman, the very essence of what, in this context, the word 'liberal' means. The concern for it differentiates the civilised person – the gentleman, as he often calls him, to our perhaps barbaric ears a little quaintly – from the savage. Knowledge as such will not necessarily make people morally better; it will not necessarily provide them with jobs; it will not turn them into Christians. Newman had no doubt that people should be encouraged to improve morally; they should be trained for useful work in appropriate ways; they should be helped to Christian faith: all very sound purposes, but none of them is as such the purpose of the university. 'The Perfection of the Intellect' he declares

> ... is the clear, calm, accurate vision and comprehension of all things, as far as the finite mind can embrace them, each in its place, and with its own characteristics upon it. It is almost prophetic from its knowledge of history; it is almost heart searching from its knowledge of human nature; it has almost supernatural charity from its freedom from littleness and prejudice; it has almost the repose of faith, because nothing can startle it; it has almost the beauty and harmony of heavenly contemplation. (I. IV. 6)

These words from the sixth discourse, like our earlier quotation from the lecture given three years later on Scientific Investigation, present an almost mystical image of a university's nature. Is this really still a fallen world? Newman seems at his least theologically gloomy about human nature in such passages. The university appears as, almost, an alternative way to overcome the Fall. Take away the five 'almosts' from our passage and we are left with a quite triumphalistic statement about what could only be the bride and Body of Christ, a supernatural creation. The 'almosts' remain but how close they still leave this high point of nature – a British university – to the realm of grace!

Newman is not proposing in theory or in fact a useless university, symbol of an effete impractical liberalism. He knows very well that young Dublin Catholics will have to earn their bread and butter soon enough. He is only putting first things first. Of course, he recognises that the great universities of the past had their professional faculties – Law, Medicine, even Theology – to follow on after Arts. Of course, he insisted that 'If a liberal education be good, it must necessarily be useful' (I. VII. 5) – useful in itself, creative, prolific, reproductive.

> Educated men do what illiterate cannot, and the man who has learned to think and to reason and to compare and to discriminate and to analyze, who has refined his taste, and formed his judgment, and sharpened his mental vision, will not indeed at once be a lawyer or a pleader, or an orator, or a statesman, or a physician, or a good landlord, or a man of business, or a soldier, or an engineer, or a chemist, or a geologist, or an antiquarian, but he will be placed in that state of intellect in which he can take up any one of the sciences or callings I have referred to, or any other for which he has a taste or special talent, with an ease, a grace, a versatility, and a success, to which another is a stranger. (I. VII. 6)

All this the genuine university needs to keep in mind as much today as then. The most successful school in Newman's university was, in practice, probably that of medicine but, in theory, he wants the university's 'practical end' to be conceived primarily in far more general terms. It is no less than 'training good members of society', 'cultivating the public mind', 'purifying the national taste', 'supplying true principles to popular enthusiasms', 'giving enlargement and sobriety to the ideas of the age' (I.VII.10). Would we now dare admit to aiming so high?

I would like at this point to consider the applicability to ourselves of two small passages from *The Idea* which reflect prophetically on aspects of our current predicament. 'Great men,' he claims (they are people in power with whom he does not agree), critical of the fact that universities cannot demonstrate the immediate usefulness of all the work they do in a narrowly utilitarian way, 'argue as if everything, as well as every person, had its price; and that where there has been a great outlay, they have a right to expect a return in kind' (I. VII. 2). What is there 'to show for the expense of a university?' What a very contemporary question! It is not unreasonable to relate work to cost and, heaven knows, universities are now being relentlessly obliged to do it. Nevertheless, unless we continue to believe in a university which has a unity of purpose and intercommunion, beyond being a mere cluster of cost-effective resource centres, the university such as we have known it and as Newman analysed it, will be lost.

It is fascinating to see Newman more than once use the word 'intercommunion' – that rather specially ecclesiastical word – to interpret the internal nature of the university, the co-operative relationship of distinct disciplines. Thus, in our second text, from the lecture on Scientific Investigation, he describes a function of the university as 'to effect the intercommunion of one and all; to keep in check the ambitious and encroaching, and to succour and maintain those (subjects) which from time to time are succumbing under the more popular or the more fortunately circumstanced; to keep the peace between them all' (II. VIII. 2). There are clearly Virgilian echoes here and Newman does indeed go on to quote Virgil's 'Tu regere imperio populos, Romane, memento' and to argue that what an empire is in political history, a university must be in the world of the mind. It must succour and maintain disciplines temporarily in peril from succumbing to the pressure of the times. Is that too not apt?

It is this sense of a shared responsibility for the whole of knowledge, this intercommunion of the disciplines, which Newman stresses as central. It is an ideal which, at least until recently, we have mostly taken for granted. Admittedly, it is impossible to teach everything – all languages, all technologies, the history of all countries. The very explosion of knowledge in the second half of the twentieth century has forced us to recognise the necessity for a self-denying ordinance in some quarters, for arrangements to spread the burden between universities in regard to the less popular, or even the most expensive of subjects. Sometimes rationalisation may require the closure of departments without any sense of treason to the ideal. Yet it does appear that since the 1980s universities in Britain have taken two different roads on this central issue and that one of them leads directly away from Newman's *Idea*.

I worked in the University of Zimbabwe from 1982 to 1985 at a time when overall numbers were increasing by some five hundred a year but the number of white students (still a majority until only a few years earlier) was falling fast. Certain subjects had been taken almost only by whites, among them classical languages, Portuguese and Afrikaans. By 1983, three years after Independence, all these areas were in serious trouble. There was no longer a Professor of either Classics or Modern Languages and – seeing the shortage of posts to cope with swollen numbers in many other departments – voices were naturally raised arguing for their abolition. I was a member of the Faculty Committee appointed to consider the issue. What struck me was how strongly the view was held that these subjects should all be retained, even Afrikaans, which at the time had not a single student. The university's new black leadership and also senior officials from the Ministry of Education all took the view that it would be wrong because of present circumstances to narrow the range of the university's scope. The subjects involved were judged to have importance for the retention of the sense of totality required by a university. If at present little sought after, surely that could change (it has, I am told, in fact already significantly changed). Academic intercommunion requires, in Newman's view, that the university succour subjects temporarily out of favour. Zimbabwe agreed.

Not so, alas, Aberdeen, where I was Lecturer and Reader from 1976 until 1982. The Aberdeen of 1976, presided over by Sir Fraser Noble, was a university in which one could actually still feel and pronounce with enthusiasm that line of local poetry

> What marvellous mad hopes were cherished
> In Aberdeen!

It was indeed, by historic destiny, the intellectual capital of a distinguished region. As a mere Englishman, I found it exciting to see my class assemble of boys and girls from Orkney and Shetland, Skye and Rum, Inverness and Montrose. There were Glaswegians too, and even a few Sassenachs; but for me, at least, it was the sense of sharing in the integrated academic life of an institution which endeavoured to provide everything for its region, and which had done so for centuries, which made it so exciting. The Scottish mixing of students in their first two years across departments as well as the four-year MA course, the fairly small scale of the university and strong regional identity, combined with the very architecture of Old Aberdeen to give one a very special sense of community. It still seems to me to have come rather close to the Newman ideal. Yet, inevitably, many of its very varied departments were small and only too vulnerable to the knife of a very different philosophy. What do we see today? It used to be entertaining to pass by the portals of the Department of Natural Philosophy and remember that elsewhere the subject was known as Physics. For no very good reason the title was then changed to Physics, but now the department itself has disappeared, to survive, it seems, only in a service role for Engineering. Upon the Arts side the list of casualties is quite horrific: the History and Philosophy of Science, Russian, Scandinavian Studies, Italian and Portuguese, Music;

even, and most hard to bear, Classics, one of Aberdeen's original chairs of almost five hundred years.

In this example, as in several other places, the ideal of Newman, the sense of the maintenance of a rounded totality of intellectual concern, the obligation to succour small subjects, seems to have been lost; one hopes, remembering Aberdeen's long history, but temporarily. However hard it may be, I cannot see any greater or more humane responsibility for university leadership today than to recommit itself to the Newman ideal and to a refusal to go down the road of reshaping universities by a policy of brutal amputation, governed by the norms of immediate financial profitability or particularised research potential. Our self-understanding should be higher and more holistic than that.

Let us now return to the tension present within Newman's own handling of his *Idea*. One perhaps sees it best of all in the eighth discourse entitled 'Knowledge viewed in relation to religion'. Quite accurately, I believe, yet still surprisingly, Newman here asserts that academic life, genuinely lived, tends naturally to create a sort of 'religion of its own', intellectually and morally attractive, superficial perhaps in terms of the more inward and supernatural of religious virtues, yet arguably more successful in producing courtesy, truthfulness, gentleness, amiability, a sense of justice than Christianity itself.

Near the end of this discourse comes the famous passage on the virtues of a gentleman. It begins with the near definition that he is one who never inflicts pain and continues with a description of great sensitivity. This is Newman's conception of the sort of person a university will naturally produce. It seems a splendid conception and one may easily be misled into reading it as a highly Christian one. Consider, then, the most unexpected yet, surely, most deliberately selected example of the type he has in mind: none other than Julian the Apostate. How baffling a selection for 'the pattern-man of philosophical virtue'. It is really rather extraordinary that the Christian theologian, having built up sympathetically his model and ethic of an institution to which he is in some way so profoundly committed, and in terms so elevated that one may hesitate to follow him, then distances himself from it all so decisively by selecting as its hero a figure so deeply antipathetic to the Christian. No wonder Newman preferred to return to the Oratory, one might say, but that would be to misjudge the subtlety of his theology of the relationship of nature to grace and his own commitment to both.

Are we then into the business, the Irish bishops might ask, to produce not saints, not even soundly educated devout Catholics, but rather a multiplication of Julians: gentlemanly philosophers too subtle quite to believe? It is indeed a paradox. Newman enjoyed paradoxes; he loved a certain rhetorical excess. But he is very consistent here. Church and civilisation are not and cannot be the same thing. The university is the quintessential institution of the latter, nature at its best, but that is always an 'almost', inherently ambiguous in its immediate fruits, as the world always will be, but utterly unavoidable. If the church is really confident of itself, he says, it should wish to meet nature at its best and most sophisticated, far more awkward a sparring partner as it then must be. A first class university will never be an easy companion for the church, it may immediately prove a quite contentious one, but it is still immensely to the church's long-term gain to be able to work in and with such a milieu.

Newman is being intensely honest here and in being so is surely risking his whole enterprise. He is trying, as a Catholic churchman, to persuade Catholic churchmen to back a genuine university while making very clear that it is of the nature of a university not to do quite what you expect of it, not to be the docile, hierarchically-controlled institution Rome certainly had in mind. 'Give us the money but trust us to do the job in the only way we honestly can' is what Newman is really saying; 'It can not be a tool of church or state or business'. A seminary or a business school is not a university. University man as he was, Newman was still more a churchman. His testimony, despite its many qualifications, is all the more valuable for that. And also, I believe, the more valuable for us. He looked at 'a university, viewed in itself, and apart from the Catholic Church, or from the State, or from any other power which may use it' (I. VI. 2).

If we are to apply Newman's message appropriately, we need to be able to carry it across from a university/church situation to a university/state or a university/business one, the 'any other power'. The principal point of his book appears to me an appeal to the church to recognise the nature and overwhelming value of a university, despite a university's intrinsic inability to be both faithful to itself and to fulfil the church's every immediate wish. A university is infinitely more valuable, he is saying to the bishops in a certain necessary awkwardness, than as a utilitarian tool of catechesis and Catholic morality, important as these are. Unlike an institution of professional training, he urges again and again, it needs 'time' and 'elbow-room' to produce its fruits. It is a thing of its own, comparable with empire or church, in a way the very greatest thing in the whole world of human life and intelligence. You may work within it to 'direct the current' (I. IX. 9). You cannot, you must not, utilitarianise its purpose in the interests of anything else whatsoever, or belittle the freedom or range of its totality. Are we prepared to say the same to our paymasters of today?

A lecture given in Glasgow University, for the Newman Centenary
3 May, 1990.

NOTES

1   *Autobiographical Writings*, p. 286.
2   Owen Chadwick, *Newman*, p. 56.
3   *Autobiographical Writings*, p. 259.
4   *Letters and Diaries*, XIV, p. 364.
5   *Letters and Diaries*, XV, p. 71.

William Temple

A man so broad, to some he seem'd to be
Not one but all Mankind in Effigy:
Who, brisk in Term, a Whirlwind in the Long,
Did everything by turns, and nothing wrong,
Bill'd at each Lecture-Hall from Thames to Tyne
As Thinker, Usher, Statesman, or Divine.

Ronald Knox's well-known lines describing Temple in his satiric poem of 1912, *Absolute and Abitofhell*[1], the Chaplain of Trinity's response to *Foundations: A Statement of Christian Belief in terms of Modern Thought, by Seven Oxford Men*, have all the brilliance of Oxford disputation at its best, mingling the profound, the personal and the comic. Temple was just thirty at the time but, thirty-five years later, would it have been less appropriate to speak of him as 'all Mankind in Effigy who ... did everything by turns and nothing wrong'? The friendly sarcasm of the Chaplain of Trinity had become, or remained, a strangely apt account of the man whom, when he became Archbishop of Canterbury, Bernard Shaw could describe as 'a realized impossibility'.

Who was this prodigy? Born in 1881 in the episcopal palace of Exeter, he moved as a child from there to Fulham Palace and then, once more, to Lambeth Palace when his father, Frederick Temple, became Archbishop of Canterbury in 1897. By then William was at school at Rugby, where his father had long been headmaster in pre-episcopal days, and where his godfather, John Percival, was headmaster when he began his schooling. Frederick was sixty when William was born and an autocrat. 'Father says so' was the decisive rule of his childhood but it seems not to have been a rule which bound him in any way he found irksome. Both his father and his very aristocratic mother greatly loved him and he responded with the profoundest *pietas* which, indeed, he kept extending to other father-figures in his life – to Percival, whose biography he in due course wrote, rather boringly; to Randall Davidson, who succeeded his father at Lambeth; to Bishop Gore, whom he described as the one 'from whom I have learnt more than any other now living of the spirit of Christianity'[2]; and to Edward Caird, Master of Balliol when William arrived there. Caird succeeded Jowett and Frederick Temple had been at Balliol with Jowett. It was all of a piece.

William was quintessentially the perfect heir of late Victorian ecclesiastical and academic education at its most perfect, and the totally grateful heir. He never had an unkind word to say about it or about the great patriarchal figures who had towered over his youth, whom he venerated unstintingly but who seem never in the slightest to have intimidated him. Benign *pietas* was coupled in youth with an equally benign – almost conceited, it seems so confident – exploration of the mystery of all things, philosophical, religious, historical. Asked by his tutor at Rugby to write an essay on ghosts, and told that it was too theological, he reports back to his father 'I asked Cole how one could discuss "Ghosts" without being theological and he only said it was not what he wanted. He also said some people would object to my discussing St Paul's vision and a banshee under one head, but I made him confess that that was because they do not think.'[3] 'As regards Berlioz' *Faust*, I think you would understand it', he could write patronisingly to his mother at sixteen.[4] Fat, everlastingly good-humoured, with a passion for strawberry jam and strawberry ices, this very superior know-all might appear a quite insufferable schoolboy but as he enjoyed at Rugby the most distinguished teaching and only left school when aged over eighteen and a half, he had by then acquired an intellectual sophistication far beyond the average undergraduate of today.

At Oxford he experienced for a little while a mildly rebellious mood. His early intentions to be ordained came slightly under question and he could write, as he hoped sounding rather radical, to a friend that

> the doctrine of the Incarnation, permanently present in its true purity to Browning, is hopelessly mauled by nearly every clergyman who touches it . . . the Christ men believe in and worship is to a great extent a myth and an idol – very different from Him who lived and died 'to bear witness to the truth', and whose Spirit lived and spoke

in Socrates and Buddha and Mahomet as it did also in Hosea and Luther and Browning.[5]

By 1905 he had been President of the Oxford Union, had published an essay on Browning, become a Fellow and Lecturer – principally on Plato's *Republic* – at Queen's College and joined the Workers' Educational Association, of which he would soon be President. His theologically radical days were nearly over. Late that year he could already write

> To be at one with the Church in fundamentals is vital. On the other hand ... it is not quite easy to see what are fundamentals ... It is the great wisdom of our church that it was not founded to support any particular doctrines, as the Protestant bodies were ... freedom in doctrine is the life-breath of the Church of England ... What I have been taught to regard as the fundamentals do seem to me strictly continuous with my philosophy.[6]

He still hesitated about Virgin Birth and Bodily Resurrection, but not very greatly nor for long and in 1908 he was ordained a Deacon in Canterbury Cathedral by Randall Davidson, acting very clearly as Archbishop and as successor to Frederick Temple.

Temple read omnivorously but one wonders how much formal theology he bothered with. He claimed when still quite young to have read St Thomas' *Summa Theologiae* through from beginning to end. I confess it is the only thing he said about himself which I have found quite hard to believe, but it may explain why in later life his almost intuitive convictions about war, property or natural theology came to have such a Thomist look to them. Nevertheless the creative minds whose thoughts most stimulated him and to which he kept recurring throughout life were, apart from the New Testament, Plato, Shakespeare, Browning; not the Fathers, not the Scholastics, not the Continental Reformers of the sixteenth century, not even the great Anglican divines of the seventeenth, not finally the biblical critics of his own age for whom he had very little time. He was, perhaps, characteristic of the modern Anglican theological temper, in being so much more shaped by literature and music than by theology. Music was very important; it had been so at school and remained so. He was fortunate in having a splendid singing, as well as speaking, voice, a voice for liturgy, for preaching, for lectures, for the conversation with everyone which was so central an activity of life and which was so frequently intermixed with his extraordinary laugh.

There can be no question that for many people Temple's laugh remained the most precisely memorable thing about him. Already at school he was remembered for 'that queer high laugh that went on so long and never left him'[7] and which would be referred to sometimes with irritation, more often with delight, throughout his life. He once laughed so loudly and continuously at a performance of *John Bull's Other Island* that Tawney, who was with him, began to wonder if they would be asked to leave the theatre. A human being, it may be said, is actually definable as an animal that can laugh – at least a passage in the *Summa* rather suggests that.[8] It is Temple's humanity in all its subtlcty which revealed itself in the sheer range and quality of his laughing, but it could certainly be concentrated with particular delight upon certain subjects. When he got away for a few days holiday with his wife just as the Second World War was about to begin, he was reading her *Alice Through the Looking-Glass*. Limericks were especially favoured and he once compared Bishop Gore's taste in limericks with his own. Gore, it seems, enjoyed something fairly simple, like this:

> There was an old man of Calcutta
> Who had a most terrible stutter;
> 'G-g-give me', he said
> 'Some b-b-b-bread
> And b-b-b-b-b-b-butter'.

Temple felt that this achieved the absurdity which a good limerick is meant to express at the cost of being, linguistically I suppose, not 'quite fair'. Temple, on the other hand, greatly admired the following against which Gore, he tells us, 'vigorously protested':

> There once was a gourmet of Crediton
> Who ate pâté de fois gras; he spread it on
> A chocolate biscuit
> And said, 'I'll just risk it';
> His tomb gave the date that he said it on.[9]

What seems to have tickled Temple here was not only the complicated rhythm but an altogether more subtly absurd story-line clinched by its terrible *dénouement*.

The laughter was just a natural part of someone on the surface always extraordinarily relaxed, friendly, 'simple' in manners, wholly unpretentious, never 'rattled', never confrontational, never angry. He became an archbishop who liked to stand in bus queues and open his own front door, to chat with anyone he encountered and at a level of profound equality and openness. He really did lay all his cards on the table. When praised by a speaker in a vote of thanks for being the greatest and simplest of Archbishops of York, he could not help but burst forth 'God, who made me simple, make me simpler yet.' When students at Leeds greeted him with 'Where have you been all the day, Billy boy?' he could not resist responding at once 'Well, if you must be so personal, I spent most of the morning with an archdeacon, and before that I did my letters with my secretary.' When Gore and Temple once walked away from a meeting at Church House, which had had to be adjourned because Gore had lost his temper, Temple was his usual genial, smiling self and Gore remarked bitterly 'I have a vile temper. It is a terrible thing to have a bad temper.' But then, looking at his companion's smile, he added 'But it is not so bad as having a good temper.'[10]

Behind all this lay a photographic memory, an outstanding fluency with the English language, an unruffled life of prayer, an often pretty ruffled flow of enthusiasms, and a quite unflagging sense of personal vocation as teacher and priest. 'William propounds the wildest plans at breakfast,' remarked his mother when they were living together, 'but he has generally forgotten them by lunch time.'[11] That quotation presents us with a useful hinge for advancing now a step or two in a new direction. Very perfect and equable characters rather tend to be dull. If Temple unquestionably avoided dullness through his extraordinary sense of enthusiasm and interest in every side of life, how far could that enthusiasm get without turning confrontational? Gore had had the enthusiasms but was confrontational, Davidson avoided the enthusiasms and held the church together, but was very dull. Temple's problem always would be how to carry enthusiasms through to achievement without, meanwhile, breaking any eggs.

Any adequate evaluation of Temple is up against a number of considerable hurdles. The first is the effusively laudatory character of almost everything written about him. There was an undiscriminating degree of praise on the part of his numberless ecclesiastical followers which does not help one to sift the grain from the chaff. On some accounts it would seem a belittling and unfair disparagement to suggest that there could be any chaff around at all. This is not helped by the inadequacy of the one official biography. Nothing, perhaps, is needed more for the religious history of Britain in the twentieth century than a really major new biography of Temple. It would certainly not be easy to write but, without it, there are large holes in the canvas. It would need to consider very subtly such matters as a lack of sustained sense of direction despite his quite frenetic activities until he was forty or more, the depth of his grappling in the 1930s with Fascism and Nazism, his relationships with Bell and Tawney. I feel an underlying worry as to whether Temple was ever critical enough of his own image, or whether in a way he came to be dangerously bamboozled by the more superficial side of his own extraordinary successes.

Michael Ramsey, a great admirer of Temple, once remarked of his predecessors as judges of character: 'Cosmo was flawless; Temple was hopeless; Fisher was superb; I am erratic.'[12] If Temple's judgement about people was poor, it seems probable that the same was true in regard to situations. One feels that all his geese were swans, especially (but by no means exclusively) all the important people he continually met in church and state. One feels that he was somehow disarmed by the sheer goodness and affability of his own heart. Hence while he could proclaim a crusade before he had really approached a situation, once he was in it he tended to be very over-conciliatory. Take the example of his brief period as headmaster of Repton. When elected by the school governors in 1910, he had written what has been termed a 'revolutionary' letter about the way the public schools still seemed to 'reproduce our class-divisions in accentuated form'[13] and what he hoped to do if they actually wanted him. 'If they take me, knowing this, I come', he wrote, threateningly enough, to Ford, his predecessor. They took him. He went and rumours were aroused: 'What form would the revolution take and what would be the first moves?' But nothing much happened, other than a change of music master, and Iremonger revealingly comments: 'As term followed term with no rocking of the foundations, it began to be suspected that there was to be no revolution after all. The suspicion proved to be well founded, the revolution never came; Temple's experience had led him to change his mind.' As a member of the Repton staff, D. C. Somervell, explained

I remember Temple telling me, near the end of his last term, that when he wrote the revolutionary letter, his ideas of public school policy were of the vaguest: a mixture of boyhood recollections and

WEA Utopianism. As he said to me on that occasion – 'If there is
one thing my time has taught me, it is that institutions must be run
on their own lines or else scrapped'.[14]

I believe the Repton episode is far more of a parable for Temple's whole
career than is usually admitted. I suspect that when he helped mount the
'Life and Liberty' campaign with such ringing, revolutionary words, he
had little more idea as to how the Church of England worked than in 1910
he had had about public schools. I also doubt whether he had any real
sense of the plight of the industrial poor or what they were up against
when in 1924 he called together COPEC (Conference on Christian
Politics, Economics and Citizenship) or endeavoured to negotiate in the
later stages of the Miners' Strike; and I doubt whether he had any very
sharp sense as to what was going on in Germany in the 1930s or, say, the
British wartime policy of obliteration bombing. Perhaps his later pleasure
in opening his own front door derived secretly from the absence of any of
the normal experiences of a common man, unswathed in palaces, public
schools and Oxford colleges. When he went to Canterbury, an admiring
journalist, Sidney Dark, admitted that Temple preferred 'to inspire the
revolutionaries rather than to lead the fighting at the barricades'.[15] That
was kindly put and Dark may not be saying anything so very different
from William's mother's remark that his 'wildest plans at breakfast' had
generally been forgotten by lunch. That was Temple and it would be
quite mistaken to argue otherwise, to prove him an effective reformer, a
man who could administer revolutionary change or whatever. He wasn't,
being someone open to rather easy conviction that 'institutions must be
run on their own lines', and it is only when we clearly recognise he wasn't
that we may begin to recognise too what he really was.

Better than anything else he was a teacher. His huge flow of
schoolboy letters to his parents constituted the first great expression of
his irresistible urge to explain, to pass on to others lucidly, imaginatively
and agreeably the knowledge and insights he had himself just attained. At
Queen's lecturing on Plato, at Repton in his readings of *Lear* and *Hamlet*
or in his sermons, in writing *Mens Creatrix* and *Christus Veritas*, in his
radio talks or the famed university missions he gave, we see always the
same: not so much a scholar, a theologian, or even primarily a leader, but a
mind committed to communicating a vision with infectious enthusiasm –
'the magic fascination of the love of Christ' as he called it to the boys of
Repton. That was what he wanted Repton to instil, what he always and

everywhere wanted to instil. There was exceptionally little difference, I think, between Temple the lecturer and Temple the preacher. His lectures always led to a more obvious religious and moral conclusion than we quite care for these days, while his sermons tended to range over things and sources well beyond what preachers were expected to do – the urge to link together St Paul and the banshee never left him.

It was a vision of wholeness. To a quite exceptional extent what Temple was always concerned with, both in his major writings and in his addresses of all sorts, was a coherent account of total experience, a dialectical account which worked through tension and contrast to expose the central meaning of things in the Incarnation. It was always moral, always philosophical, always Christ-centred. Here was a man, highly conscious of the secularising, the disintegrating but also very much the pessimistic tendencies within society and culture around him. He could not yield to them. It was almost a weakness of his spirit to remain so cheerfully optimistic, so determined to harmonise the philosophy of dialectical idealism, the socialism he saw advancing across the world, the literature, art and music of Europe he had so profoundly imbibed, into a vast incarnational synthesis. The Incarnation for Temple, as for Scotus, did not derive its meaning from the need for redemption, it was rather the inevitable and perfect crowning in grace of the whole order of things in created nature.

More and more as the years passed, the central purpose of Temple appears as this one: a theological teacher for a wide public but certainly not a theological scholar. As such he had no peer. No Archbishop of Canterbury since Anselm could conceivably be compared with him in this regard, no bishop of his own age. Despite the lack of time he had in which to write the principal books of his later years, one suspects that they do not suffer greatly as a result. He would not have improved them through a larger availability of scholarly space because he never had been that sort of scholar. It was always as a teacher, at the interface of his faith and other people, that he shone, but this very incarnational dimension of his own work – the hereness and nowness of his teaching – makes it inevitably less satisfactory for anyone of a later age, unable to share the spell of Temple's unique here and now: of that moment, to give just one instance, at the end of the great Oxford mission of 1931, when in a crammed St Mary's he stopped the singing of 'When I survey the wondrous Cross' before the last verse and asked the students present to read the words first and then 'if you mean them with all your heart, sing them as loud as you can. If you don't mean them at all, keep silent. If you mean them even a little, and want them to mean more, sing them very softly.' Suddenly two thousand voices whispered together:

> Were the whole realm of nature mine,
> That were an offering far too small;
> Love so amazing, so divine,
> Demands my soul, my life, my all.

It was an experience never to be erased from the memory, but Temple's teaching time and again did produce a comparable experience in his listeners and in a huge circle of followers who across the next generation of Christian life in this country would look to Temple in a way that they never looked to anyone else, and in a way that since his death there has been no one else quite to look to. He had the authority and immediacy of a prophet but was the content of his teaching truly prophetic?

It is truer to say of Temple than of most people that he never changed. His qualities were already extraordinarily apparent as a boy at Rugby both to his contemporaries and to us. Yet the very precociousness of his genius retarded, I believe, his maturity. The same might be said of other public school and Oxford geniuses of that delectably precious age, Ronald Knox especially. One has for years a feeling that Temple could not quite grow up and did not really want to. Even the First World War, while it made him more than usually over-active, did not mature him very noticeably. It is difficult to demonstrate such things but my impression is that his passion for meetings, addresses, missions, campaigns, only begins to give way to a cooler sense of pastoral responsibility as the central dynamo within his system well after he became a bishop in 1921 and still more noticeably after he moved to York in 1929. The archbishopric of York may have been the one entirely suitable position he occupied in life. The trouble of the pre-1921 years had been the number of quite different jobs he had accepted and abandoned. York was right for him. Here was a *cathedra* for teaching, national, even international, rather than for formal ecclesiastical administration and political involvement.

He was too briefly at Canterbury, and in the quite special circumstances of war, for us to be able to appraise him very satisfactorily as Archbishop of Canterbury. It was, of course, right that he should be translated from one to the other on Lang's retirement. He had no rival. And it is not true, as Henson claimed, that if he had lived he would have found he had outlasted his eminence: on the contrary. The post-war world would have suited him admirably and his role in it as the great presider and spokesman of the enlightened consensus in matters religious not only for Britain but for the United States, Europe and the World Council of Churches would, undoubtedly, have been outstanding – a role no one person after his death could ever fill. Chairmanship was certainly one of his *forte*s. Nevertheless it remains true that he was weak in the political and administrative skills, manoeuvring within the corridors of power, which an Archbishop of Canterbury most needed, and that he was strongest in the more essentially public and oratorical skills of a ministry of teaching; personal, at once philosophic and popular, episcopal without doubt but more than ecclesiastical, a ministry which can really be exercised better at York than at Canterbury.

The York years are those on which above all Temple should be judged and they are the years of his three most valuable books: *Nature, Man and God*, his Gifford Lectures 1932–4, *Readings in St John's Gospel* and *Christianity and Social Order*. It is especially through these that Temple will endure, if he does endure, and it is from them and other contemporary evidence that we can best enter into his mind at its most profound. To help us here I will compare four passages from that last decade of his life which reflect upon the way he saw himself and the theological predicament about him.

The earliest is from the Preface to *Nature, Man and God*, dated June 1934. He first describes two types of thinker. The first lays out all he knows about a subject and 'piece by piece will work out his conclusion'. The second type, the intuitive, is the one to which Temple saw himself as belonging:

> All my decisive thinking goes on behind the scenes; I seldom know when it takes place – much of it certainly on walks or during sleep – and I never know the processes which it has followed. Often when teaching I have found myself expressing rooted convictions which, until that moment, I had no notion that I held ... This characteristic must needs affect the philosophical method of him who suffers (or gains) from it ... The two types described – are they the Aristotelian and Platonic, the Pauline and Johannine, respectively?

In his personal Introduction to the *Report on Doctrine in the Church of England* which he composed in October 1937, there is a slightly different dualism. The first part of the century, in which his own mind was formed, had concentrated upon 'a theology of the Incarnation rather than a theology of Redemption'. A theology of the Incarnation, he continued,

> tends to be a Christocentric metaphysic. And in all ages there is need for the fresh elaboration of such a scheme of thought or map of life as seen in the light of the revelation in Christ. A theology of Redemption (though, of course, Redemption has its great place in the former) tends rather to sound the prophetic note; it is more ready to admit that much in this evil world is irrational and strictly unintelligible ... If the security of the nineteenth century, already shattered in Europe, finally crumbles away in our country, we shall be pressed more and more towards a theology of Redemption ... It is there that, in my own judgement at least, our need lies now and will lie in the future.

My third text is from the Preface to the First Series of *Readings in St John's Gospel*, dated December 1938:

> For as long as I can remember I have had more love for St John's Gospel than for any other book. Bishop Gore once said to me that he paid visits to St John as to a fascinating foreign country but he came home to St Paul. With me the precise opposite is true. St Paul is the exciting, and also rather bewildering, adventure; with St John I am at home.

Finally, a passage from an article he contributed to *Blackfriars* in March 1944.[16] Here he contrasted two approaches to the theology of Aquinas, the first holding it decisively mistaken, the second

> that his map needs correction in some important respects but that our most hopeful line of advance is to start with his work, making such corrections as we think it needs. To which of these two groups we belong is likely to depend on our admitting or repudiating the possibility of natural theology and the value of analogical argument from created nature, including human nature, to the nature of the Creator. It is not sufficiently understood in England that on the European continent this more than anything else is the point at issue

between Catholicism and Protestantism. The Continental Reformers had so interpreted the Fall of Man as to leave in fallen human nature no capacity for recognising divine truth ... In my own mind there is no doubt on which side of that division we should stand.

These four passages share something of a common structure. Each presents a contrast between two approaches or theologies; with one of which (type A) Temple each time identifies himself. In the first, type A is characterised as intuitive, Platonic and Johannine; type B, argumentative, Aristotelian and Pauline; in the second, type A is a theology of Incarnation, 'a Christocentric metaphysic', type B a theology of Redemption, stressing the irrational and the prophetic. In the third text, type A is Temple at home in St John, Paul a bewildering adventure; type B Bishop Gore at home in Paul, a foreigner to John. In the fourth text, type A is Catholic Thomism stressing natural theology and type B Continental Protestantism stressing a fallen world and no human capacity for recognising divine truth.

Different as these four dualisms may seem in some ways, I feel fairly sure that they are really, for the mature Temple, all of a piece. His theology throughout has been the Incarnational one fed on Plato and John, a Christocentric metaphysic which plays back and forth between nature and supernature, stressing the intelligibility and goodness of things, no need to be prophetic, but finding especially in later life that what had started out as idealism was ending up as Thomism, and what had seemed a species of liberal Protestantism, beefed up a bit with a dose of mainstream Anglicanism, was really a kind of classical Catholicism. In contrast he sees Paul and Gore and Barth, a theology of Redemption, the admission of a sinful crazy world, the call to prophecy rather than to philosophy, essentially the theology of Protestantism. It may seem rather too odd to claim Gore as the Protestant prototype, Temple the Catholic. I suspect there is a good deal in such an evaluation objectively enough, but the point is that it is how Temple was coming to read himself and his theological position.

Of course by the late 1930s he is having his doubts. Barthianism seems to be spreading all around him. Too much in the world, he sees, simply has not got the intelligible character he had learnt to find in it with late nineteenth-century optimism. He clings to Natural Theology and Natural Law, is glad to find that as Hegel slips away he can turn instead to Thomas but somewhat alarmed at the seemingly rather irrational, almost

Barthian, character of some of the young Anglican Neo-Thomists he meets.

In his Introduction to the *Report on Doctrine* he goes so far as to suggest that theology really needs to be moving away from his kind, type A, back to the other kind, but he was recognising too that if this was a need to be met by younger theologians, he himself could do little. 'I doubt if I can now *lead* them' he admitted, 'perhaps I might do a little in steering them ... But is it really the function of an Archbishop to be a theological leader?'[17] About the same time as he wrote that, a letter to Dorothy Emmet in July 1942 suggests a way in which rational and irrational might cohere:

> What we must completely get away from is the notion that the world as it now exists is a rational whole; we must think of its unity not by the analogy of a picture, of which all the parts exist at once, but by the analogy of a drama, where, if it is good enough, the full meaning of the first scene only becomes apparent with the final curtain; and we are in the middle of this. Consequently the world as we see it is strictly unintelligible. We can only have faith that it will become intelligible when the divine purpose, which is the explanation of it, is accomplished.[18]

This he claimed was already there in *Nature, Man and God* but the total impression had remained static rather than dynamic. In this letter to Dorothy Emmet he seems closest to transcending the dichotomy between two approaches which he had himself set up, while still trying dialectically to defend the substance of his own ground. We see him in these last years coming a little sadly to recognise the non-contemporaneity of his own approach, though it may be that very much more of his approach did remain valid than the next generation was inclined to think. Certainly it is sad that Temple of all people should be driven to question whether an archbishop should be a theological leader. Of course almost no archbishop ever has been, but that is just where Temple seemed different. If the sense of crisis, sin and unreason unrooted him from his Idealist origins, it did not take him from St John and he could find in the fourth gospel, within his theology of Incarnation, a theology also of Redemption, darkness and prophecy. Take this splendid comment from his *Readings* on John 1:5 (7–9):

> The divine light shines through the darkness of the world, cleaving

it, but neither dispelling it nor quenched by it ... It is always so. Take any moment of history and you find light piercing unillumined darkness – now with reference to one phase of the purpose of God, now another. The company of those who stand in the beam of the light by which the path of true progress for that time is discerned is always small.

Remember Wilberforce and the early Abolitionists; remember the twelve Apostles and the Company gathered about them ... As we look forwards, we peer into darkness, and none can say with certainty what course the true progress of the future should follow. But as we look back the truth is marked by beacon lights, which are the lives of saints and pioneers; and these in their turn are not originators of light but rather reflectors which give light to us because themselves they are turned towards the source of light ... This darkness in which the light shines unabsorbed is cosmic. St John is most modern here ... He does not conceive of Nature as characterised by a Wordsworthian perfection, which is only spoilt by fallen mankind. To his deep spiritual insight it is apparent that the redemption of man is part, even if the crowning part, of a greater thing – the redemption, or conquest, of the universe.

In these words we hear Temple facing the darkness of the late 1930s, so different from the 19th century security in which he had been brought up, with a deep alteration in mood still more noticeable in a little article, 'Theology Today', published in *Theology* in November 1939[19] in which, almost for the first time he recognised, as a true prophet, that we do indeed 'peer into darkness':

We have to face this tormented world, not as offering a means to its coherence in thought and its harmony in practice, but as challenging it in the name and power of Christ crucified and risen; we shall not try to 'make sense' of everything, we shall openly proclaim that most things as they are have no sense in them at all. We shall not say that a Christian philosophy embraces all experience in a coherent and comprehensive scheme.

In the darkness of war he seems here almost to repudiate the writing of a lifetime. Yet it may be precisely at that point that his positive insistences move from optimism to prophecy. Already he was wondering whether a

Thomist scheme might not, after all, provide a new 'starting point' and, anyway, he remained sure that 'one day theology will take up again its larger and serener task and offer to a new Christendom its Christian map of life, its Christocentric metaphysic'. Even in that day, Temple was soon busy once more attempting some part of that 'map of life' with his *Christianity and Social Order*, perhaps the most enduring of his works. Here again he is dipping into the natural, stressing natural law, stressing the sort of rational order to be expected and sought in a divine and Christ-centred universe. The *Theology* article can best be seen as a moment of purification, in which the philosopher's naturally Johannine vision is forced to become Pauline as well.

> A man so broad, to some he seem'd to be
> Not one, but all Mankind in Effigy.

We have seen something of Temple's lifelong realisation of what was intended as a caricature. He retained his passion for synthesis to the end, appealing in the last year of his life for 'a new integration of life: Religion, Art, Science, Politics, Education, Industry, Commerce, Finance'.[20] He retained too his optimism, his ability even while still 'in the middle' to see beacon-lights in the present and not only from the past. Thus his Enthronement sermon at Canterbury on St George's Day 1942 centred quite optimistically on 'the great new fact of our era', the Ecumenical Movement, whereby far from 'returning to the catacombs', the City of God 'again stands before us with gates wide open so that citizens of all nations may enter'. In some way, his repeated dualistic division of theological roles excluded him from Paul, prophecy and Protestantism. By and large that seems correct: Temple so often claimed as a prophet was not naturally one at all, unlike Gore or Bell. Yet we cannot simply place him, as he often placed himself, upon the other Johannine, intuitive and harmoniously philosophic side. These binary categories really won't quite stand up on their own account, let alone when someone as broad as Temple is placed against them. Maybe archbishops are not theological leaders, yet he undoubtedly tried to be one and no one in this country since Anselm more nearly succeeded. Temperamentally he was not a prophet, but many people found him stunningly prophetic.

Michael Ramsey, the only other good Canterbury claimant to such a role, was invited as a young theologian to Bishopthorpe by Temple in July 1936 with a galaxy of names – Emil Brunner and Reinhold Niebuhr,

J. H. Oldham and Visser't Hooft – to help plan the ecumenical conferences of 1937. Ramsey came greatly to admire Temple but he admired Gore too and if at one time he thought Gore old-fashioned and Temple more contemporary, later he thought Temple dated and Gore still authoritative 'with the mysteriousness of a timeless authority'.[21] Theological fashion has its ins and outs. What is certain is that the three greatest theological names in twentieth century Anglicanism have been Gore, Temple and Ramsey. Temple remains the man 'in the middle', his time cut off in war, still the most enigmatic of the three, the most difficult to make up one's mind about. Yet when Ramsey was asked where he wished to be buried he replied 'I should like to be not far from William Temple.' Some of us, I believe, would be glad to say the same.

A lecture given at Keble College, Oxford,
in the John Keble Bi-Centenary Lecture Series,
12 May 1992

NOTES

1 'Absolute and Abitofhell', first published in the *Oxford Magazine*, reprinted in Ronald Knox, *Essays in Satire*, 1928, pp. 81–8.
2 W. Temple, *Studies in the Spirit and Truth of Christianity*, 1914, Dedication.
3 F.A. Iremonger, *William Temple*, 1948, p. 22.
4 Iremonger, p. 31.
5 Iremonger, pp. 102–3.
6 Iremonger, p. 106.
7 E. V. Knox, Iremonger, p. 35.
8 Aquinas, *Summa Theologiae*, III, q. 16, a. 5.
9 W. Temple, *Religious Experience*, 1958, p. 189.
10 A. E. Baker in *William Temple: An Estimate and an Appreciation*, 1946, pp. 109, 95, 98.
11 Iremonger, p. 67.
12 O. Chadwick, *Michael Ramsey*, 1990, p. 118.
13 Iremonger, p. 147.
14 Iremonger, p. 148.
15 Sidney Dark, *The People's Archbishop*, 1942, pp. 108–9.
16 Reprinted in *Religious Experience*, 1958, pp. 229–36.
17 Iremonger, p. 608.
18 Iremonger, pp. 537–8.
19 Republished in W. Temple, *Thoughts in War-Time*, 1940, pp. 93–107.
20 W. Temple, *The Church Looks Forward*, 1994, Preface.
21 P. Avis, *Gore: Construction and Conflict*, 1988, p. 4.

6

English Catholicism in the Late 1930s

No age in the modern history of English Catholicism has, I suspect, fallen into greater oblivion than the later 1930s. There are certain recognisable high points in English Catholic intellectual history, such as the Second Spring and the subsequent long ascendancy of Newman and Manning, the years of the modernist crisis prior to the First World War or, again, the zenith of Belloc, Chesterton and their friends after the war. Certainly, for many years for good or ill, the Chester-Belloc dominated the scene, but GK died in 1936 and Belloc's creative period was long past. Finally, subsequent to the Second World War, the scene changes dramatically with major institutional and numerical growth, linked to the inauguration of the welfare state, heavy Catholic immigration, an immense schools programme and the emergence on a considerable scale of an educated Catholic middle class.

There were various reasons why the later 1930s and their particular atmosphere faded rather fast from the collective consciousness, and yet they possessed a singular brilliance of their own – if a partially tainted brilliance – which it is worth recalling. They witnessed indeed what can fairly be called a little renaissance, if one destined to be swept away fast enough by the winds of world war and state socialism.

The fears and counter-fears engendered by the modernist movement and its repression undoubtedly produced in this country as elsewhere a somewhat arid piece of intellectual history in the twenty years subsequent to *Pascendi* and it was only as the 1930s wore on that, at last, a certain relaxation of institutional tension became apparent coupled with a very considerable infusion of new blood. A number of able young cradle Catholics were joined by a veritable spate of glittering converts; some of these had admittedly been received a good deal earlier but they had initially kept fairly quiet. By the mid-1930s they seem to have acquired the sense of a *droit de cité*, encouraged by the best leadership in the religious orders and the very much improved openings for published work. There developed the very strong sense of a Catholic intellectual community, self-confidently speaking of 'the Catholic revival', sunning itself in country houses or at Campion Hall, publishing its books with the young Frank Sheed, its articles in the revivified *Tablet* of Douglas Woodruff or the *Catholic Herald* of Michael de la Bedoyere, drawing in new members from the worlds of letters, art and even academia.

English Catholicism continued to suffer in this decade from the social split between a small, rather consciously English upper class elite and the urban working class, concentrated in Liverpool and the other larger northern towns, with its strong Irish connections. There was still little sense of cultural or political identity between the two – their subsequent drawing together would depend upon the wider social revolution of the post-1945 years. The renaissance of the 1930s remained wholly inside the small, mostly upper-class 'English' segment, which was a major cause of weakness. It was only possible at all because of a fairly steady enlarging of that class which had been going on in connection with a growth in professionalism in the public schools. This was the great age of Downside, Stonyhurst, Ampleforth and their companions, the age of the headmasters who were near national figures – Sigebert Trafford, Paul Nevill, Ignatius Rice. These schools would continue to grow in subsequent decades but the far greater growth in good grammar schools after 1944 would steadily diminish the overall ecclesiastical significance of the boarding schools. But without them the world of Ronald Knox's Oxford chaplaincy and Woodruff's lay-orientated *Tablet* and Frank Sheed's annual list of Maritain and Mounier, Martin D'Arcy, Gerald Vann and Sheed himself would hardly be imaginable.

It remained, nevertheless, from the side of its home writers a predominantly amateur world, with many of the characteristics of a gentleman's club. It still participated only marginally in the life of a university. Stalwarts like Francis (Sligger) Urquhart at Oxford and Edward Bullough in Cambridge – two pillars of Catholic life to die in 1934 – had not seen it as their role to provide any very public sort of intellectual leadership, and the small though growing group of Catholic academics that followed them presented an almost equally low profile. What had been done was to prepare the way internally, through the development of a relaxed chaplaincy system and a general diminishing of prejudices, for the vastly enlarged Catholic presence in the universities of the next generation. In the 1930s the most striking sign of such a presence was Martin D'Arcy's new Campion Hall in Brewer Street, something of a Mecca for converts. 'I slipped along Brewer Street like a homing pigeon', wrote Frank Pakenham of his conversion.[1] D'Arcy was by far the most influential clerical intelligence of the decade. It is likely that since Newman no other priest has exercised so deep and prolonged a personal influence upon the English Catholic intelligentsia, and behind the glittering eye of the living Jesuit was the still more pervasive influence of the dead Jesuit.

The 1930s were the decade of the belated triumph of Gerard Manley Hopkins. It opened with the second edition of his poems published in 1930 with an introduction by Charles Williams. That was really the moment at which his unique distinction was recognised by a now admiring world and new impressions followed year after year. Little as the Society of Jesus had appreciated his poetry in his lifetime, it now possessed an added charism in his reflected glory. Listening to Martin D'Arcy reading *The Wreck of the Deutschland* could be a spiritual experience not easily forgotten. Despite D'Arcy's close links and deep sympathy with the gentlemen apologists who were so much in their zenith in those years, his new Campion Hall was a powerful and intended pointer towards the far greater intellectual professionalism which was soon to come.

D'Arcy himself could qualify without question as a theologian, as could one or two of the men at Blackfriars nearby, but there were remarkably few people of weight, priest or lay, who could honestly be so described in the English church at the time. Such as existed were centred upon the three institutions of Downside, Blackfriars and Campion Hall. These three had all in fact nourished young men of great ability and scholarly capacity who were just beginning to make their mark by the late 1930s – David Knowles, Christopher Butler, Victor White, Gervase Mathew, Frederick Copleston. To them should be added the seculars, David Mathew and Philip Hughes. They constituted a new and highly promising class of professional priest scholar whose weight would be strongly felt in the post-war years.

Among priests of the previous generation perhaps only Dom Hugh Connolly had achieved a comparable professionalism within a deliberately restricted academic field. Apart from D'Arcy the distinguished priestly names of the 1930s – Ronald Knox, C. C. Martindale, Vincent McNabb, Bob Steuart – were neither theologians nor professional scholars. They were 'men of letters', radio priests, preachers of genius, on their way to being gurus, but they had maybe lived too long beneath the modernist shadow to show any desire to stray far into the silent garden of the queen of the sciences, to which they paid an infinite wary deference.

The Catholic world of the later 1930s was, then, one with few recognised theologians, academics or professional scholars. It was a world, moreover, which had emerged, not from the discipleship of Newman or Acton or even Von Hügel, but rather from the swelling circle of Belloc and Chesterton – and Belloc far more than Chesterton, perhaps because Belloc had been a Roman Catholic all the time and his spirit harmonised a great deal more readily with that dominant within the church of this period. It is indeed odd that a Chester-Belloc unity was ever imagined because, whatever might have been the impression given to their non-Christian disputants, from within the household two more different versions can hardly be imagined. If one can somehow conjure a very clerical polarity with a very lay one, and one within a nineteenth-century context with one of the twentieth century, it is not – I think – entirely fanciful to see Chesterton as standing somehow within the religious tradition of Newman, while Belloc wore something of the mantle of Manning. Again, if the Sheeds were central to the articulate lay Catholicism of the 1930s, both inheriting the immediate past and striking out in new directions, Maisie was undoubtedly the disciple of Chesterton, Frank of Belloc.[2]

It remains somewhat strange to the present generation how widely Belloc was accepted as the master and father figure. His vast literary output over forty years of ceaseless writing could indeed father almost any form of literature and a very wide range of political viewpoint.

> Hilaire Belloc
> Is a case for legislation *ad hoc*
> He seems to think nobody minds
> His books being all of different kinds.

The Bentley Clerihew was only too much to the point. If much of his work was wholly unmemorable, quite enough of it was very much the reverse, be it mostly from his early years: one can think of the *Cautionary Verse*, *The Modern Traveller*, *Danton* or *The Servile State*. The Belloc of the 1930s was not creative in that way, but he still somehow maintained his ascendancy by the vastness of his knowledge and the forcefulness of his opinions – and not only among amateurs. It is worth noting that the group of men who produced the essays for his 72nd birthday included several professional Oxford historians. That group is indeed worth listing as suggesting something of the core of the Catholic intellectual world (minus its Jesuit wing) at the end of the 1930s: Douglas Jerrold, Ronald Knox, Douglas Woodruff, Arnold Lunn, C. A. J. Armstrong, Christopher Hollis, Gervase Mathew, David Mathew, J. B. Morton, W. A. Pantin and David Jones.

Certainly the Belloc line had been stamped strongly enough upon a whole admiring generation as the Chesterton 'line' (if one could speak of one) never was. Belloc had almost wholly ignored the New Testament and theology; in turn poet, historian, essayist, fringe politician, he was an apologist almost all the time. The post-Bellocian Catholicism of the 1930s was moulded very strongly in this image. It had nearly always an underlying apologetic quality, be it in the writings of the Sheeds, of Alfred Noyes, Arnold Lunn, Edward Watkin, perhaps even Christopher Dawson, though these and their contemporaries were gifted men and their apologetics took many a form, some of it very low-keyed. With Knox, perhaps the most brilliant of them all, it could remain four-fifths hidden in a self-deflating 'all this waste of time' – not a wholly misguided comment on even so superbly devised a piece as *Let Dons Delight*.

What remains striking is the sheer quality, above all the literary quality, of the published work of this period at its best. What other five years could, from this viewpoint, rival those which saw the publication of Waugh's *Edmund Campion*, David Jones's *In Parenthesis*, Knox's *Let Dons Delight* and Graham Greene's *The Power and the Glory*? But these masterpieces (three of which won the Hawthornden Prize) were backed by a very considerable body of work, much of it of some distinction: *The Celtic Peoples and Renaissance Europe* of David Mathew, Christopher Dawson's *Making of Europe*, *Voltaire* of Noyes, Maisie Ward's *Insurrection versus Resurrection*, Rosalind Murray's *The Good Pagan's Failure* and Tolkien's *The Hobbit*! One could easily continue the list: poetry, fiction, history, apologetics, but only the hint of anything which could really be called theology.

Maisie Ward, who had made the second volume of her father Wilfrid's biography, *Insurrection versus Resurrection*, into a wide-ranging survey of modernism, ends it with a triumphant epilogue hailing the end of 'the siege period' when it would at last be possible to utilise 'all that was really valuable in the thought of the Modernist period'.[3] Algernon Cecil, reviewing the book in the *Tablet*,[4] noted that it 'is instinct with the sense of a great change in the Catholic outlook', her epilogue 'falls upon the ear like the sound of a reveille warning the faithful that it is now indeed high time to awake out of sleep'. To a reader of today that reveille still heartens, even if it does sound a little simplistically triumphalist; a too confident belief in 'Christian civilisation'.

There was a good deal of highly stimulating philosophy coming across the Channel in those years. It was the age of Mounier and Maritain, many of whose works were circulating in English translation by the late 1930s. Maritain was probably the most wholesome major continental influence on English Catholicism at the time, and the most firmly anti-Fascist one. His work was a major stimulus for Dawson, Gill, the young Barbara Ward among others. But he too was careful not to appear a theologian. The 'new theology' of Congar, De Lubac, Danielou and the like hardly reached England before the war, though the less challenging work of Masure and Mersch had done so. In the strict realm of theology as in the theory of church government an Ultramontanism of the latest Roman vintage was simply unchallenged among the clergy and followed *faute de mieux* by the laity and every fervent convert. Manning and his successors really had done their work very well. The English Church was now Ultramontane in its thinking through and through. It is striking but unquestionable that even the ablest of its younger priests, men whose wider culture and historical sense could have brought them to a different theological viewpoint, were unmitigatedly Ultramontane. One can think of David Knowles, David Mathew and Christopher Butler. Only in a few lay people such as Maisie Ward or Edward Watkin, Donald Attwater, Alfred Noyes, Malcolm Hay or Robert Sencourt, is there some hint of a different vision of ecclesiastical order.

The most characteristic contemporary practical expression of the Ultramontane system was the development of that organisation which came to be known at the time as 'Catholic Action': a centralised, Rome-inspired, hierarchically-controlled, model for the mobilisation of the laity. To the Ultramontane mind it was the appropriate response to the new restlessness of the laity and the new apparent powerlessness of the clergy in the socio-political field, and it was really greatly preferable to any 'Catholic party' because the latter had at least theoretical and potential independence from clerical control which Catholic Action could never have (the willingness of Ultramontanes to sacrifice the Popular Party in Italy and the Centre Party in Germany was only too clear). Catholic Action was, by definition, lay participation in the hierarchy's work under the hierarchy's control – essentially it was devised as a brilliant but absolutely necessary foundation stone within the twentieth-century context for the whole Ultramontane edifice, and it was hailed in the 1930s by English Ultramontanes as just what the times required. Father Philip Hughes put the whole thing with maximum clarity: 'Catholic Action is the layman's movement, but its success presupposes a laity adequately trained and in some measure specially organised. The chiefs of the movement are, everywhere, the bishops. Never again will the Church have to face the trouble that came of an extra-diocesan, extra-hierarchical Catholic organisation where the effective direction of Catholic activity passed to elected committees of clergy and laity'.[5]

Not surprisingly it did not work very well in England. Despite the *Tablet's* natural denial that it was 'merely a cunning form of Fascism',[6] that is how it only too easily appeared, particularly in view of the Fascist sympathies of so many of the more vocal British Catholics. But perhaps more important than the somewhat Fascist image was the absence of a suitable ecclesiastical or political environment. If the Catholic Church in this country was at that time almost irretrievably Ultramontane in the theological presuppositions of its clergy, it was not so by any means (and this fact is often completely overlooked) in its wider structures or social attitudes which shared far more in the general pattern of contemporary Britain. From this point of view there was a very striking contrast between British and Dutch Catholicism – the latter had developed an Ultramontane-inspired society in a way the former had not done despite Manning's hopes. There was neither Catholic university nor daily newspaper, neither political party nor trade union. Elsewhere such institutions provided much of the grounding for the large scale activities of Catholic Action. Moreover, the rather sharp cultural and political divide between the small Catholic middle class and relatively large working class inhibited common action except upon the straightest ecclesiastical or moral issue. There was, as a consequence, an airy unreality about the campaign to get Catholic Action going.

An imaginative native English development such as the Catholic Evidence Guild was quite clearly something very different, and it steered pretty clear of the social and the political despite a strange appeal from one Sheed & Ward author for 'new apostles' who would be 'in the natural order, the propagandists of Fascism, and, in the supernatural order, the lecturers of the Catholic Evidence Guild'.[7] While 'the young movement of Fascism' would work 'that England may attain the happiness of authority in the Corporate State', the 'young movement of the Catholic Evidence Guild' would work 'that England may attain the happiness of authority in the Corporate Church'.[8] It may seem almost unbelievable today that a Catholic publisher who was very far from a crank could produce such rubbish in October 1937 – still more so as the publishers in question were also the leaders of the Evidence Guild and could hardly publish something about their own cherished organisation if they thought it incredibly dangerous or misleading. Here as elsewhere Ultramontanism was proving itself an easy bedfellow with Fascism. But in practice the profound residual Cisalpinism of English Catholicism rooted in common sense, supported by the wider national society and quite unbewitched at the working class level by the myth of 'Corporativism', either politely disengaged itself from Catholic Action altogether or transformed it into something very different from Cardinal Pizzardo's model.

A *cause célèbre* of the workings of the Ultramontane system and its limitations may be found in the curious incident of the action of the Holy Office over Alfred Noyes' study of Voltaire, which was published by Sheed & Ward, serialised in the *Tablet* and widely acclaimed by reviewers. The book was then secretly delated to the Holy Office and Cardinal Hinsley was abruptly informed that it would be condemned if it were not withdrawn from publication until its errors had been eliminated. The publishers at once dutifully complied with this and they had, at first, the agreement of the author. What the errors consisted in was neither then nor later officially revealed and the whole business quickly stuck in the author's gullet and a fierce correspondence broke out in *The Times* in August 1938. Noyes decided to republish the book in its original form with another, neutral, publisher and this was seen by some as 'Defiance of the Holy Office', though Hinsley did his best to damp down the acrimonious heat and was able to declare a year later that, after all, no alterations whatsoever would be needed in the book.[9]

Other people had judged differently. The reaction of Noyes to the action of the Holy Office had caused both admiration and dismay. 'It is quite impossible to sympathize with his impatient appeal to the Protestant public', wrote Denis Gwynn of Noyes in the *Dublin Review*.[10] The readers of *The Times* were thus labelled 'Protestant' rather than simply a section of fellow citizens. With a few exceptions Catholics showed an almost complete inability to face up to the deeper issues of the case. At the time they simply had not the tools for mounting a challenge to Roman behaviour precisely on Catholic principles. Instead, if the Holy Office would not point out errors, there were industrious fellow Catholics who set about doing so. They came up with dozens of them. Noyes had described a respected eighteenth-century bishop as an 'old imbecile' – how could the censors be expected to pass so offensive a phrase? He had argued that Voltaire, though by no means a Christian, had had a more Christian conception of God than some of his ecclesiastical opponents and had also behaved at times in a more Christian fashion. 'There is something not only Christian, but Christ-like, in the reply of Voltaire', he had written at one point. Such a comment, Gwynn thought, was 'unjustifiable and offensive' and the sort of thing no proper ecclesiastical censor could be expected to put up with. To be fair Gwynn, while playing the Ultramontane game, by no means shared the Ultramontane objective: the firm subjection of all and sundry to the Roman curia. On the contrary he was, somewhat deviously, hoping to demonstrate pragmatically that a Roman system of censorship just would not pass with sturdy British authors. The system, as Noyes had clearly shown to the chagrin of some and the secret delight of others, could only be upheld so long as it was not challenged. Once this happened the Ultramontane house of cards started to tumble and something had to be done. While the church was certainly not ready for its official dismantling, it could do little else on pragmatic grounds than turn a blind eye to its partial disregard by the laity. In practice the latter was unprepared to follow an Ultramontane line very far either over 'Catholic Action' or over the control of literature, but in theory it offered little support to Noyes in his appeal as a matter of principle to a deeper 'law of religion and the Church' (*The Times*, 20 August) over and against canonical procedures of censorship and suppression.

Fascist sympathies and ecclesiastical Ultramontanism were different attitudes and did not need to combine; nevertheless they were both at home in English Catholicism at the time (as they were in Italian Catholicism), they had a good deal in common and could in fact rather easily reinforce one another. The one derided liberal parliamentary democracy as Protestant in inspiration, degenerate and phoney, and lauded Latin and Mediterranean political experience as more genuinely democratic (of a populist kind), Catholic and 'counter-revolutionary'. The other wholly subordinated local church to Rome and laity to clergy as a matter of divine law. Both tended to prefer Latin models to Anglo-Saxon ones, and obedience and order to freedom and public debate.

The Spanish Civil War broke out in July 1936 and lasted until March 1939. It proved a decisive catalyst in the parting of contemporary loyalties – far more so than, say, the mounting anti-Jewish campaign in Germany – and it placed almost all vocal English Catholics, clerical and lay, emphatically on Franco's side. Eric Gill and his circle were pretty isolated in their pro-Republican sympathies and even 'left-wing' *Blackfriars* did no more than try to keep an open mind either way.

'No sane and instructed man would hesitate to prefer Fascism to Communism', declared the *Tablet* in an important editorial in February 1939. Even at that late date it appealed to Catholics 'not to join or encourage this anti-Fascist crusade'. A few years earlier David Mathew had observed that 'Politics play little part in the Catholic community as such, except in the circle of the Distributists.'[11] Yet there was a dominant political orthodoxy among vocal English Catholics in the 1930s which is quite unmistakable. Douglas Jerrold was probably its most reliable proponent. On a bedrock of Conservatism – the Jesuits and the Benedictines had long seemed to vie with one another as to which could more fittingly be described as 'the Tory party at prayer' – there was a continual harping on the positive values of Fascism, and the mystique of 'the Corporate State'. Here, too, much was owed to Belloc. Despite a very real radicalism in his youth and a capacity for trenchant political observation which never wholly deserted him, Belloc had settled with the years for the dream of some sort of righteous populist dictatorship. Sneers at liberal democracy and anti-Semitic jokes had become part of the stock-in-trade of too many a vocal Roman Catholic. Theological Ultramontanism was for a while fairly easily harnessed to a cultural and social Ultramontanism which at first hailed Mussolini, and continued to hail Franco and Salazar, as the finest expressions of the Catholic political point of view. Only a tiny minority of English Catholics shared Maritain's refusal to support the Nationalist cause in Spain and to see both the Spanish Civil War and the wider crisis of Europe in the very simplest terms as a conflict between Christianity and Communism; while the anti-religious atrocities committed by the Republican side were harped on ceaselessly, next to nothing was said about the still more numerous atrocities committed by the Nationalists, and little more about the persecution of the Jews elsewhere.

The case of the acute amateur Scottish Catholic historian Malcolm

Hay is worth recalling at this point. While his early books (in the 1920s and 1930s) were immensely well received by Belloc and English Catholics because they most effectively punctured various segments of British Protestant historical myth, things were quite different when Hay proceeded to analyse with equal vigour the Christian tradition of anti-semitism. He at once lost almost all his English Catholic friends. As he wrote in 1950: 'My own personal experience tells me that all my Catholic friends (with three or four exceptions) are infected to some degree. They are therefore unable to take an objective view of the Jewish Christian problems which their ancestors have created. I had a small circle of English Catholic 'friends' including several well-known English Jesuits. All those people dropped me completely ...'[12]

Frank Sheed, as we have seen, could in 1937 still publish a book which thought it helpful to consider the Catholic Evidence Guild and the Fascist Movement as parallel forces for righteousness. The same book, *Fascism and Providence*, which made that suggestion, declared of the Nazis, 'The Pope has not pronounced against the Nazis – on the contrary he has a concordat with them, and upwards of a million of the four million Nazis are Catholics, and Catholic Bavaria is their particular stronghold and birthplace. Fascism, in fact, is of Catholic origin and no English Catholic has a scintilla of right to condemn the Nazis. Catholics who do, and there are some few who are busying themselves considerably, may be found to be fighting against God'.[13] Dom Christopher Butler, reviewing the book in the *Downside Review*, while mildly critical of some of the author's positions, commented 'The English public see the most unlovely features of so-called "Fascism" out of all proportion to those profounder qualities which have rallied to it so much of the best elements in western and central Europe'.[14] Even in June 1938 the *Month*, while asserting that Hitler 'now serves under the banner of anti-Christ' could still continue (p. 483): 'Of the four great European powers only Italy and Germany have taken the menace of atheist Communism seriously, realizing that if it gets further foothold in Europe it will make an end of law and order and of civilized life. It is undoubtedly a pity that those two states are totalitarian, and themselves interfere unduly with the natural liberties of their subjects, but in opposing communism they are fighting the battle of the democracies as well.' It is only too clear that even in 1938, in the majority judgement of the English Catholic intelligensia, 'civilised life' was not as such threatened by Nazism and Fascism but only by Communism.

Nevertheless there was always an alternative voice. If Vincent McNabb's holy simplicity somehow suggested within the vocal clergy of the 1930s an 'alternative society' to the establishment world of D'Arcy and Knox, a voice without a Tory accent, his friends from the old Ditchling community represented in their different ways an alternative lay voice to country house quasi-Fascist sympathies. The hard clarity, indeed ruthlessness, of Eric Gill's often idiosyncratic convictions challenged prevailing Catholic orthodoxies at almost every point: on sex, on pacifism, on seeking an anarchic rather than a corporatist model for society, on anticlericalism, on Communism. 'A Christian politic should always be one which leads in the heavenly direction, looks to anarchy as its guiding star', he wrote in September 1936.[15] He was confronting here the whole profound Catholic presupposition that 'law and order' in church and state was what Catholics should be most concerned to maintain. His critique of Communism could be sharp enough and public enough but he had no doubt that 'between Communism and Fascism I'm all for Communism',[16] thus asserting a position which was anathema for almost all his co-religionists; he was even prepared on occasion to associate with Communists and, for doing so, received more than one delicately communicated admonition from Hinsley – though Catholics who associated with Fascists would surely not have been so treated! He was quite impenitent.

Gill's disciple and intimate friend, David Jones, drawing on much the same sources of guidance on the Catholic side – Maritain and Dawson and their Blackfriars friends – forged a less trenchant, more enigmatic, more decisively creative body of writing. Both in watercolour and in words, Jones's mastery was somehow in locating a very concrete here and now foreground within a perspective of almost unfathomable, yet still human, depth and mystery. That after all is what the Mass, his central point of reference, is all about. A seer where Gill was a prophet, he wove a vast web which convincingly located the war, the fight against tyranny, the immediate predicament, within the central cultural tradition of Europe, expressed by the figure of Arthur in one way, the Latin liturgy in another.

The late 1930s were Gill's last and greatest period both in artistic achievement and in vigour of thought – the time of his superb bas-reliefs, 'The Re-creation of Adam' under the opening words of *The Wreck of the Deutschland*, 'Thou mastering me God', in the League of Nations Council Hall at Geneva. In such work, as in Jones's *In Parenthesis* or

Chesterton's extraordinarily perceptive but almost unknown poem *Ubi Ecclesia*, English Catholicism really was manifesting a sensitive Catholicity fully faithful to the best in its heritage and very different from the corporatist flag-waving which too often passed as sound Catholicism in those years.

At the time Gill and Jones must have seemed marginal enough, if not cranky, though they were not without their immediate circle of influence: the pressures and anguish of the time were forcing people in more than one direction. They certainly represented an apparently less typical side of English Catholicism, but then so did Newman, so did Hopkins, so did Von Hügel, so – despite the acclaim he received – did Chesterton. If the English Catholic tradition in modern times can be characterised by a certain rather heavy keeping in step at the centre, it can be characterised too by the number of highly creative figures it has sprouted in its margins. Moreover, though they seemed more or less marginal at the moment, such people have time and again proved not to be marginal at all on the longer view but rather the unexpected bearers of an authentic spiritual continuity.

While the later 1930s were all in all an important and exciting moment within this tradition – a moment of renewed confidence, even of brilliance, whose literary output was very considerable, and in which a serious challenge to the narrow clericalism and unadventurous thought patterns of the post-Manning and post-modernist eras was at last beginning to be mounted, it has to be admitted that its achievement has been largely swept into oblivion, and from the seeds sown the harvest was seemingly slight. There were various reasons for this. One, clearly, was the effect of the war and of the major social changes which followed it. Another was the increasingly restrictive attitude of church leadership in the age of Griffin and Godfrey not only in this country but also in Rome. The latter years of Pius XII's reign, symbolised better than anything else by the encyclical *Humani Generis*, were not ones really to encourage Catholics to feel, as Maisie Ward had suggested, that 'the siege period' was now over. But there were as well decisive causes inherent within the very nature of what was achieved in those years of Hinsley and Pius XI. There was the amateurishness of so much of it and its rather narrow, almost cliquish, social base. Still more serious, there was the almost criminal blindness to the evils of Fascism stimulated by an all-engrossing opposition to Communism. The fondness for Fascism derived not only from an 'enemies of one's enemies are one's friends' logic but also from two other sources – a natural sympathy for Catholic southern Europeans from Italy to Portugal and decades of Bellocian indoctrination about the fraudulency of Western democracy and the perils of Semitic influence.

When the war came and the country found itself called to fight for democracy and against Fascism, Catholics responded as well as anyone else – their sympathies had never been very pro-German anyway. In doing so they had inevitably to bury much of the sentiments of the pre-war years and they did so remarkably easily. What remained of that thinking after 1945 might seem little beyond a lobby for Salazar and Franco which lingered on for decades, coupled with the sort of rather phoney nostalgia which hangs so heavily over *Brideshead Revisited*. The Catholic intellectual community was about to be reformed on the basis of Butler's Education Act and such sentiments would seem to the new generation of Catholics increasingly odd and uncongenial.[17]

Beyond the flirting with Fascism and the Ultramontane theology there was, however, as I have suggested, a great deal of more solid value as well as literary brilliance, together with a training of new minds, and all this was not lost. If some of the figures who appeared central in the 1930s never seemed subsequently able to escape from the mental limitations of the dominant Catholic model of that period, others certainly did so, pursuing new courses with both integrity and creativity. Among clerics one may well think of Christopher Butler – so much more of a prophet in the 1960s than in the 1930s – among lay people Maisie Ward, perhaps the most homely and characteristically English figure of the pre-war renaissance; she would sail confidently on to welcome the age of the priest-worker, the Second Vatican Council and aspects of *aggiornamento* amazingly remote from the preoccupations of the 1930s.

Then again they were the years in which David Knowles was writing what may well have been his finest volume, *The Monastic Order in England*, which so clearly marked him out as the ablest English Catholic historian since Acton and destined him soon to be appointed to Acton's old chair – the Regius Professorship at Cambridge. They were the years in which Tolkien was getting down at Oxford to work on an epic of vast imagination, very different in formal structure but not so dissimilar in inspiration from that of David Jones – *The Lord of the Rings*. And they were the years in which Barbara Ward made her appearance as a social thinker and reformer. From a grounding in Maritain and Dawson, she was to go steadily forward as one of the great prophets of our time – a person as difficult as any to fit within the normal stereotype of English

Catholicism. Finally, if the most solid intellectual achievement within the English Catholic community in the years after 1945 should be judged to lie in the far greater professionalism of its quieter, more academic proponents – mostly lay and increasingly numerous: Evans-Pritchard, Tolkien, Elizabeth Anscombe, Mary Douglas, Donald Nicholl and dozens of others, it is at least arguable that this would hardly have come about without the gentle encouragement and friendship of priests such as Gervase Mathew, Victor White and Tom Corbishley – priests whose wide horizons, sense of vocation and intellectual discipline had been acquired in those years of the 1930s when 'the siege period' was suddenly – if perhaps prematurely – felt to be coming to its end.

NOTES

1 Frank Pakenham, *Born to Believe*, Jonathan Cape, 1953, p. 97.
2 Maisie Ward, *Unfinished Business*, Sheed and Ward, 1964, p. 309
3 Maisie Ward, *Insurrection versus Resurrection*, Sheed and Ward, 1937, p. 546.
4 The *Tablet*, 18 December 1937.
5 Philip Huges, *Dublin Review*, April 1939, p. 216.
6 The *Tablet*, 2 July 1938.
7 Christopher Butler, The *Downside Review*, January 1938, p. 105, reviewing and summarising the argument of J. K. Heydon, *Fascism and Providence*, Sheed and Ward, 1937.
8 J. K. Heydon, *Fascism and Providence*, p. 153.
9 Alfred Noyes, *Two Worlds for Memory*, Sheed and Ward, 1953, p. 273.
10 Denys Gwynn, the *Dublin Review*, October 1938, p. 206.
11 David Mathew, *Catholicism in England*, Sheed and Ward, 1936, p. 261.
12 Alice Hay, *Valiant for Truth, Malcolm Hay of Seaton*, London, 1971, p. 150.
13 J. K. Heydon, *Fascism and Providence*, p. 142.
14 The *Downside Review*, January 1938, p. 105.
15 *Letters of Eric Gill*, edited by Walter Shewring, Jonathan Cape, 1947, p. 362.
16 Robert Speaight, *Eric Gill*, Methuen, 1966, p. 238.
17 See the remarks of John Lynch in the chapter on England in *The Church and the Nations*, ed. A. Hastings, Sheed and Ward, 1959, p. 9.

7

The British Churches in the War and Post-War Reconstruction

It can be helpful to consider the relationship of the churches and the political and social community in this century in the context of four large phases. While the relationship we have taken as our subject is a British one, it needs to be understood as sharing in a wider history. At times Britain has taken the lead, at times it has rather followed a trend, carried along by a larger tide. In each of these phases we need to recognise the principal secular pressures, both in terms of social and political developments and in terms of ideology, before identifying the church response to those pressures, again both in terms of action and ecclesiastical change and in terms of theology. We may be able too to discern in each case a certain cycle within the phase, a pattern of leadership, an early enthusiasm for coming to grips with the needs of the world followed by a waning of enthusiasm when the cost of the endeavour became plain, a threat of dislocation in church–state relations seemed likely, or the secular pressures themselves decreased or changed. Inevitably in all this, and not discreditably, the world set the agenda and could therefore change it. Church leaders and theologians, gearing themselves to grapple with one agenda, have tended to fall back into quietism or cliché when it dawns on them that the goal posts have been altered.

The first phase stretched from the 1880s to the First World War, the era of the Christian Social Union. The underlying secular pressure derived from the stabilisation of an industrial urban world with appalling working conditions but a rise of trade union activity and socialist theories. Church reaction is to be found in various forms of Christian socialism, most of them extremely vague, in the inspiration of Cardinal Manning and Bishop Westcott, in Leo XIII's encyclical *Rerum Novarum* and in a good deal of semi-theological writing on the social gospel. While all this affected British clerical culture in the Edwardian age, at least at the leadership level, to some considerable extent, it had little wider impact. Its content was nebulous and its influence barely affected either the Tory convictions of most Anglicans or the narrow anti-drink and anti-establishment preoccupations of the Nonconformist Conscience. Effectively the First World War swept this phase out of existence though its influence carried through to fuel its successor through Temple's COPEC conference at Birmingham in 1924 and comparable developments in what came to be called 'Christian Sociology'. For the most part they were of a theoretical and moralising character, very weakly related either to the contemporary political scene or to any specific church activity.

The second phase may be dated from the early 1930s to the mid-1950s. The secular pressures behind it were the slump and mass unemployment, the growing power of Communism and Fascism throughout the world, the Second World War and its genocidal concomitants. The church response to these unprecedented challenges to anything which could possibly be regarded as a Christian social order was shaped by the SCM, *Life and Work*, and its 1937 Oxford Conference on Church, Community and State, and the leadership of William Temple and George Bell. Of all our phases it produced in this country by far the strongest body of thought and action and its character is my principal subject. After the war it slowly faded in the age of Geoffrey Fisher as Fascism was defeated, the welfare state adopted and the relationship with Communism was stabilised through the establishment of the Iron Curtain and acceptance of the Cold War as a social commonplace. The Ecumenical Movement achieved its triumph in the establishment of the World Council of Churches at Amsterdam in 1948 but then slowly lost its dynamic momentum, tied down by its own institutionalisation and the complexities of its agenda.

Our third phase goes from the end of the 1950s to the mid-1970s. The principal secular pressure here was extra-European: the ending of empire, the threat of nuclear war, the hardening of apartheid in South Africa and the tension between dictatorial regimes, largely backed by the

West, and popular aspirations in Latin America. There was also a great deal of fuelling from the secular optimism of the early 1960s and its counterpart in the upheaval within the Catholic Church centred upon the Second Vatican Council. In Britain leadership had passed from Geoffrey Fisher to Michael Ramsey. The most influential texts were official Catholic documents like the encyclical *Populorum Progressio* and the works of Liberation Theology. This phase faded as the Catholic Church drifted back from reform to conservatism. A somewhat diluted form of Liberation Theology did, however, pass quite widely into the main stream of Christian consciousness while the focus on South Africa and the combating of apartheid continued to be important with Bishop Trevor Huddleston as President of Anti-Apartheid in London and Desmond Tutu, Archbishop of Cape Town. In other areas of concern, particularly within Britain, any sense of direction was largely lost. The attraction of a bureaucratic welfare state waned but it was not at all clear what to do about it and, while Liberation Theology appeared relevant to the southern hemisphere, attempts to adjust it to Britain were rather amateur and marginal. The gap between third and fourth phase might be located in the archiepiscopate of Donald Coggan, though if he can be used to symbolise it, he certainly did not produce it.

The fourth and final phase we are now in, and it is still only beginning. The pressures come from several sides: the triumph of a capitalism bent on enlarging the gap between rich and poor, denying the existence of social morality, and demolishing as much as possible of the post-war structures of the welfare state; the collapse of Communism, productive of a Pandora's Box out of which is jumping a mass of competing and racialist nationalisms; the threat of ecological collapse. The mid-1980s *Faith in the City* report represents the first significant expression, if limited, of a church response to this phase. Since that, there has been very little, and the main ecclesiastical tendency appears to be to run away once more from secular challenges towards a revived, more fundamentalist and more sectarian religiosity, papered over both by an appeal to the need for ecclesiastical modesty and by a surface ecumenism used to justify the avoidance of any painful analysis of contemporary reality. As yet there are neither leaders nor texts of authority to guide us in our present agonies. It is clear how little can now be expected in the social field from the new Council of Churches of Britain and Ireland. It is thus out of a situation not incomparable with that of the political world and the churches about 1933 that we look back in 1994 across a full half-century to consider how the churches coped with the ante-war, the war and the after-war, an age dominated by Hitler and then by Stalin, the supreme crisis of the central twentieth century.

If we compare our two situations, what may strike one first is how much stronger was their leadership than ours, in personalities, in harnessed academic strength, in the mobilisation of resources. At the centre of it was William Temple. Temple had his weaknesses, nevertheless as Archbishop of York in the 1930s and of Canterbury in the early 1940s he could grapple with secular reality with a consistency, an efficiency and a capacity for popularising which no church leader today could begin to match. He was not alone. George Bell, J. H. Oldham and William Paton were all people of comparable ability and commitment, able to operate each within his own domain and his own specific skills. And they were surrounded by a body of intellectuals and young SCM enthusiasts to whom they could turn both for the development of ideas and their diffusion. One can see this very well by a brief look at the Oxford Conference of July 1937. It was a highly international conference and it included distinguished continental theologians whose approach was at times noticeably different from that of its principal organisers. That the latter were almost entirely British cannot, however, be doubted, for Britain almost alone provided a coherent leadership to the burgeoning ecumenical community of a sort relevant to the immediate secular crisis. The planning and advancement of the conference owed everything to Oldham, Bell, Paton and Temple, together with Oldham's young assistant, Eric Fenn, but they could count on the support of people of the quality of Sir Walter Moberly, John Baillie, Ernest Barker, A. D. Lindsay, the Master of Balliol, R. H. Tawney, T. S. Eliot, Charles Raven and many others.

The range of topic and seriousness of treatment as demonstrated by the Conference Report, *The Churches Survey their Task*, is obvious enough, yet it has to be admitted that the fruit of the Conference is not equally evident. Its intellectual role within the process of wrenching church leadership away from the simplistic in understanding the moral responsibilities of contemporary society was very considerable within both England and Scotland. Furthermore, it decided in principle to propose the establishment of a World Council of Churches, and, many would say, that is in itself enough. It is nevertheless striking that this decision could only be realised ten years later. The spiral of decline within the civilised order was already too far advanced by the summer of

1937 for any conference to have much effect upon it. If 'The Problem of the State' was the Oxford meeting's central concern, and that with Germany in mind, no one from the German Evangelical Church was permitted to attend and Pastor Niemöller had been arrested only twelve days before the Conference opened. Maybe if the churches had had the prescience to mount such a conference six or seven years earlier, it could have played a significant part in sustaining a democratic Germany. By 1937 it could do nothing. Its warning about the nation or *Volk* that 'any form of national egotism whereby the love of one's own people leads to the suppression of other nationalities and minorities ... is sin and rebellion against God' (224) was valuable in itself but far too late.

The Conference did in fact even reveal the extent of mental and spiritual confusion within Christian ranks, above all over the issue of war between pacifists and non-pacifists, though that is to simplify. The principal president of the Conference was Cosmo Lang, Archbishop of Canterbury. Lang was not a pacifist but he was an appeaser, that is to say so long as his government did not wish to go to war, he backed that policy with almost pacifist rhetoric as the will of God, though as soon as it went to war he backed it once more in just-war terms. If anything then and now takes the stuffing out of a mature Christian response to grave injustice and aggression, it is the oscillation of the erastian, the soft nationalist, between an easy appeal to Sermon on the Mount pacifism and an easy appeal to just-war principles. No one, I fear, is better at such convenient oscillation than an Anglican bishop. Church attitudes to Nazism and the persecution of the Jews remained ambivalent largely, though not of course entirely, because of the ambivalence over pacifism. When war came, this largely disappeared. On the one side, there remained a group of fully committed pacifists including Charles Raven and George Macleod. On the other side the churches as a whole and their institutional leadership rallied to the war effort but divided over whether government policy was to be given conditional or unconditional support. George Bell declared at its start that the church must not sink into being 'the State's spiritual auxiliary'. However it was a very small minority he led which was prepared so to challenge the state on failure to respect the principles on account of which going to war could alone be justified, while William Temple was ultimately, it seems to me, unprepared to be decisively more than an erastian leader. Only manifest willingness to be out of step with the Foreign Office can, in war or peace, justify the existence of Lambeth

Palace in genuinely Christian terms. Perhaps of all archbishops in this century only Michael Ramsey might have been willing so to act.

Bell proved different. His pre-war attitudes were admittedly ambiguous. His horror of war, his distress over the Treaty of Versailles and his inability to recognise how evil Nazism was kept him too long as a somewhat confused appeaser. It was only with the war that his fearless and critical freedom was really displayed – and it almost certainly ensured that when Temple died, he was not considered to replace him. Never, perhaps, has a bishop of the Church of England challenged the government so emphatically over secular policy on moral grounds, particularly in regard to our refusal to offer any encouragement to the German opposition to overthrow Hitler and our policy of obliteration bombing. Temple was not prepared to voice such concerns though he did speak emphatically about the need to do everything possible to save the Jews. In this, however, while he was criticising the reality of British policy he was not attacking the public pretence as to what British policy was. In theory, government too wished to save the Jews. In practice the Foreign Office blocked every attempt effectively to do so. Temple led the church in a nation at war, focusing positively on the future, but never publicly at odds with the establishment of power.

Bell was, the more evident, a prophet. In the words of Ulrich Simon, '... *contra mundum*! Bell led a rational, moral, realistic, fight with the world.'[1] In this he certainly did not represent the soft centre of the visible church. Nevertheless as Bishop of Chichester, he remained a voice of the church with institutional as well as charismatic authority. If the church can never use its institutional authority as a base on which to mount a prophetic voice which goes well beyond representation of the soft centre's current consensus, one may wonder about the justification of the former. This is not to suggest that Bell was always right: on the contrary. Prophets seldom are. Before, and at the start of the war, his record of appeasement may well have affected his credibility when he sought later to persuade the government to take the German opposition seriously.

The dilemma of Bell and many other near-pacifists was a real one. Both pacifism and appeasement represented in part a very proper reaction against the warmongery of many First World War clerics. Perhaps only people like Bell and MacKinnon who had for a time been pacifists or almost pacifists could come to support the war while remaining detached enough to challenge effectively the goals and methods a nation at war was too willing to embrace. One cannot think it a mistake that, when in 1948 the World Council was fully inaugurated, Bell was at once elected Chairman of its Central Committee. If in England his war record probably deprived him of the leadership of the church and left him for ever in the relatively unimportant see of Chichester, internationally he was recognised as having provided the nearest thing that existed in wartime to a true – more than partisan – *vox ecclesiae*.

It was easier for the churches galvanised both by the best pre-war Christian social thinking, of the Oxford Conference type, and the experience of war to turn constructively and collectively to the shaping of a post-war Britain than it was to respond to the immediate challenges of war. Here Temple surely took the lead with his chairmanship of the Malvern Conference in 1941, his *Christianity and Social Order* published by Penguin in 1942, with the working out of agreement for the Butler Education Act, with backing for the Beveridge Report and with the establishment of the British Council of Churches, also in 1942. At this time Temple was particularly close to Sir Stafford Cripps, Labour's leading intellectual on its front bench, as well as to his old friend Tawney. If the churches were not leading society at this point, they were at least keeping level with its more progressive developments. On a wide front of leadership they probably cannot be expected ever to do more than that and it is seldom that they do as much. That is the context of the Baillie Commission set up by the Church of Scotland in those years to explore 'God's Will in a Time of Crisis'. There was a creative harmony at that point between the churches in the two countries, a harmony which for a brief moment in 1941 included even Roman Catholicism. At the famous Stoll Theatre meeting of the Sword of the Spirit in May 1941, after Bishop Bell's speech Cardinal Hinsley, chairing the meeting, called for 'a plan of action which shall win the peace when the din of battle is over'. Six months later, 2 December 1941, Bell gave a talk in Edinburgh on the title 'A Single Christian Front':

> The Church is not a sort of universal boudoir where people meet at their ease and keep their minds away from serious things ... There is an intensity in the conflict with evil of which men have seldom been aware before. I see the evil in the blindness and selfishness of nations, including our own, between the two wars; I see it in the idolatry of wealth; I see it in the passive acceptance for years of the unemployment of millions, of the ill-housing of millions, of the

starvation of millions all over the world; I see it in the bitter nationalism which sets people against people.

Was he speaking in 1941 and not today in the 1990s?

Eleanor Jackson in her life of William Paton remarked that 'All the thought and energy which went into the Peace Aims Group, the Malvern follow-up and the Religion and Life weeks disappeared from church life after the end of the war ... No institutionalised forms were proposed.'[2] Is this true, and if so why did it happen? While the achievement of Christian thinking in helping prepare the way for a welfare state and the post-war world is unquestionable, the speed with which the churches went off the boil is no less clear and it can be instructive simply to list some of the factors involved.

Undoubtedly the sudden death of both William Temple and William Paton, caused in each case by sheer accumulated exhaustion, had much to do with it when coupled with Temple's replacement by Geoffrey Fisher, a man who claimed to want 'to follow in the footsteps of the two Williams'[3] but who was in fact incapable of providing, and deeply averse to, the kind of imaginative ecclesiastical participation in the larger leadership of society for which the two Williams had worked so hard. The death too of Cardinal Hinsley and the undermining of the Sword of the Spirit played their part. Here, of course, the balance is different: the intensity of mood under the pressure of war had made something briefly possible which was otherwise, in those pre-John XXIII days, apparently impossible. That points, however, to a factor of far wider import. The churches in the war were responding to intense secular pressure. When the pressure was relaxed, the vigour of church concern with the secular speedily declined. Thirdly, Eleanor Jackson claims, there were 'no institutional forms proposed'. Perhaps that is not quite fair. The British Council of Churches after all was new and could have been a far more dynamic tool than at first it was allowed to be. The SCM and the Christian Frontier Council were both very much in existence. Here too the Baillie Commission is to be noted. Nevertheless, despite the ticking over of such machinery, often quite effectively, the fact of a certain collapse seems unquestionable.

Bell, undoubtedly, was still there – the principal proponent of religious interventionism in the world of the secular. Both then and now, his role has been questioned. Donald MacKinnon's trenchant judgement is well known but bears repeating: 'The historians of the Church of

England may yet recognise that the worst misfortune to befall its leadership in the end of the war was less the premature death of William Temple than his succession by Fisher of London, and not by Bell of Chichester.'[4] We still lack any adequate over-arching assessment of the issues and personalities of that challenging time. One might compare Peter Walker's sensitive apologia for Bell in his *Rediscovering the Middle Way* with Jackson's defence of Paton's 'reticent use of letters to *The Times*' and 'a discreet word in the right ear', as against Bell 'completely oblivious to the antagonism he created'.[5] Many have accused Bell of obstinacy, provocativeness and sheer bad judgement, but one may question how far such accusations can be seriously sustained. The tensions between pacifist and non-pacifist, between Temple and Bell or between Oldham and Paton deserve a sensitivity of understanding not yet achieved. Neither Temple, Bell nor Oldham has received an adequate biography. An effective church needs bureaucratic 'pocket battleships' like Paton, so long as they have his degree of genuine vision, as well as more outspoken prophets like Bell. What was damaging was not the tension when all were at work but the lack of balancing talents when Bell alone was left in England in the front rank after the war.

It would, however, be totally mistaken to imagine Bell as an impractical prophet. His 'prophecy' was not located in an idealism apart from practicalities. It was not his ideas which infuriated so much as the obstinate particularising way in which he insisted on applying them. In the immediate post-war scene, it was above all with the resurrection of Germany that he was concerned. His eye had picked out unerringly the immediately most urgent but practicable challenge. At Stuttgart in October 1945 he was already there, standing beside German church leaders in their confession of collective guilt. A year later he presided over a famous meeting in the Oxford Town Hall on 5 December 1946, which had as its purpose the rallying of Christians to involve them creatively in the post-war political situation. There was now a Labour government. While the state was committed to grappling with the internal reform of British society more radically than had ever before been the case in this century, there were many new frontiers, above all overseas, where a lead was needed, but the social concern of the church was already in danger of decline.

The Oxford Town Hall meeting was intended to rally the ranks: a renewal of Christian social action in the post-war world. Victor Gollancz, Richard Acland and Barbara Ward were the principal speakers. The immediate resolution was to develop a new approach to occupied Germany and back Gollancz's 'Save Europe Now' campaign. From this too came the foundation of Christian Action, a ginger group organised by John Collins which was to be for the next quarter-century the most radical force within the church, concerned first with Germany, then with South Africa and racialism. As a Canon of St Paul's from 1948, placed there through the patronage of Stafford Cripps, Collins would in his way come to take over the Bell role – to be ahead of society in both discovering and campaigning for advance on its principal contemporary moral frontier. He would however never enjoy either the institutional status or the personal authority of George Bell. It was not just that he was not a bishop; it was also that the post-war church lacked any imaginative backroom boy with the stature of Oldham or Paton. Three years after the Oxford meeting, Bell convened a small committee in 1949 to consider what could be said about the world of the 'Cold War'. Out of it came *Christian Faith and Communist Faith*, edited by Donald MacKinnon and published with a preface by Bell in 1953. It probably represents the last significant expression of the central struggle of the British churches to serve the world creatively in the age of Hitler and Stalin.

Two years before the Oxford Town Hall meeting, a commission had been set up by the SCM to consider the fundamental needs and character of the university in the post-war world. It first met at St Deiniol's Library, Hawarden in 1944, but here too, late 1946 was a crucial time, with a major meeting in September in Cambridge. Led by Professor John Baillie of Edinburgh, the commission included among others three distinguished philosophers, Professor Dorothy Emmet of Manchester, H. A. Hodges of Reading and Donald MacKinnon, who gave the address at the Cambridge meeting. From it in due course emerged not only a series of pamphlets but Sir Walter Moberly's *The Crisis in the University*, published in 1949. Moberly was chairman of the Christian Frontier Council. He was also Vice-Chancellor of Manchester University and, subsequently, chairman of the University Grants Committee. What strikes one again here is the impressiveness of the people in the post-war as in the pre-war world whom the churches could turn to as their experts, policy-makers and guides. They did not cease to be there but they did soon cease to be much used.

The influence of the church at its best was not primarily a matter of any single document, declaration of policy or clerical leader. It was rather a matter of a wide on-going network of laity and clergy, bishops and academics who were sharing their concerns, stimulating one another and feeding the results both ways – into church councils on the one hand but to government policy-makers on the other. It required a combination of prophecy, bureaucracy and academic hard-headedness. A Temple or a Bell makes little sense on his own. Neither could have had the effect they did without the far less well-known figures of Oldham and Paton to prepare the ground for them, but Oldham lacked a necessary quality of confrontation – he was too much the Athenaeum liberal – while Paton lacked intellectual subtlety. To be effective both needed to be able to marshal Moberly, Lindsay, Donald MacKinnon and Barbara Ward to join them in study weekends and on public platforms. However, when Temple and Paton were dead, Oldham and Bell old, there was no one weighty enough to keep alive this intensity of networking. For Geoffrey Fisher there could be little point; such things were pointless or a threat to his own hierarchical authority rather than an essential part of the church's multi-faceted response to a changing world, though in the Suez crisis it was Fisher who challenged the government most effectively. But for the most part in the somewhat static, even conservative, atmosphere of the 1950s there seemed little need. John Collins, the young activist of the 1940s, would continue as the anti-racialist and anti-nuclear organiser of the 1950s and 1960s, but his allies would come from the margins rather than the central areas of church life.

John Baillie's Riddell lectures of 1945, *What is Christian Civiliz-ation?*, suggest well enough the maturity and range of contemporary intellectual authority of which the post-war church could make use: Jacques Maritain, T. S. Eliot, Reinhold Niebuhr and Christopher Dawson are all appealed to in support of Baillie's fundamental thesis of 'the danger that, by allowing the political and economic order to take care of itself, the Church of Christ will tragically fall short of its duty of bringing the light of the Christian Gospel to bear upon every activity of the common life.'[6] The integrity of justice with love which Baillie defends against more dualist, and pessimistic, continental theologians, is, of course, what a quarter of a century later Liberation Theologians would be asserting anew, if in a rather more confrontatory style.

When one looks back from the 1990s to the period we have been considering, what strikes one is the decline – in intellectual vigour, in seriousness and range of concern, in the willingness of church leaders to get together with academics and others to see what they can and should do about the world, and in the very existence of lively independent bodies like the SCM, the Christian Frontier Council and Christian Action. With the church as it was then, it would be inconceivable that the tragedy of Bosnia should have continued for so long with no significant church response of any sort. The British Council of Churches was founded in 1942 with just such needs in mind. What seems tragic is how its successor has been reduced to largely religious and ecclesiastical concerns, and how it is now unable to provide a society-orientated leadership to supplement or prod that of the churches themselves. The very success of agencies like Christian Aid has encouraged church people to be satisfied with a humanitarianism which is apolitical, far though that is from the intentions of Christian Aid itself.

As we enter a new and very dangerous phase of our history we could certainly do worse than turn back to consider the lessons of the period between the Oxford Conference of 1937 and the first Assembly of the World Council of Churches in 1948. These were years in which British Christians contributed immensely to the reshaping both of their own society and of the international church in the post-war age, but in which they then seem to have lost their nerve as the mental clarities engendered by war faded and ecclesiastical hierarchy ceased to see the point in a leadership which was innovative, shared, thoughtful and relevant to the immediate and changing needs of society. How today can such things be done again and soon? I cannot answer that question here. What I can say is that if the churches cannot be both more daring in the likeness of Bell and more innovative in recreating a network through which to be aware both of the problems of society in Britain and abroad, and of ways of responding to those problems far beyond anything functioning at present, then they will have nothing with which to justify their public status, an establishment of any sort, nothing to demonstrate that they are not simply little coteries of believers of no more significance to our society than any other sect. Britain will finally have ceased to be a Christian society because the churches and their leaders will have ceased to wish to have it so.

A lecture given at New College, Edinburgh in the Conference on Discerning God's Will in a Time of Crisis, 21–22 January 1994

NOTES

1 Ulrich Simon, *Sitting in Judgement*, 1978, pp. 86–7.
2 E. Jackson, *Red Tape and the Gospel*, 1980, p. 270.
3 Oliver Tomkins, unpublished journal, 28 April 1945.
4 Donald MacKinnon, 'Justice', *Theology*, March 1963, p. 102.
5 Jackson, *op. cit.*, pp. 317–18.
6 p. 54.

8

Catholicism and Protestantism

... nature always does contrive
that every boy and every gal
that's born into the world alive
is either a little Liberal
or else a little Conservative.

If grace perfects rather than destroys nature, as Thomas
Aquinas insists, we may be right not to be surprised if it too seems to
contrive that every little Christian is either a little Catholic or else a little
Protestant: the Christian life is not immune to a binary divide. Gilbert's
lines, while frivolous enough, in fact express a basic underlying reality of
political life as experienced in this country but really far more widely. A
healthy commonwealth needs the interplay between progressive and
conservative tendencies and if the Christian church is a human society
with at least some characteristics in common with the political community, it may well be that its health too requires a comparable binary
tension. If so we may start our enquiry by asserting the possibility that in
some way Catholicism and Protestantism may, as contrasting modes of
Christian belief and experience, not be simply opposed to each other as
mutually exclusive rivals but should rather be seen as required, interacting poles in an ongoing oscillation of Christian pilgrimage.

Whether that is so or not, they certainly represent two contrasting
forms which Christianity has assumed in western Europe over the last
four hundred years so that as a matter of fact little Christians have been
born into a church divided, apparently immutably, between Catholic and

Protestant, not too unlike the way in which the late nineteenth-century English child was born into a political community divided between Conservatives and Liberals.

To understand the two, however, we need to go behind that divide and explore the concept each has had of itself, and we will start with Catholicism. It is indeed the primary term with which, ultimately, both sides continue to identify. One, holy, Catholic and apostolic church. The Nicene Creed is common territory. The term 'Catholic', nevertheless, is more than one of its four ecclesial adjectives, even if it remains probably the most enigmatic of the four: the undivided church regularly named itself Catholic in a way that the other terms were not used. The word Catholic was thus accepted as somehow encapsulating the very essence of what the Christian church saw itself as being or, perhaps, becoming, coming to be. Catholicism meant universality, wholeness, Christianity incorporated into the entire range of human diversity: linguistic, cultural, ethnic, sexual, whatever, faithful to itself and yet almost infinitely variegated. The *Catholica* could be trusted because it was not particularist. It represented the whole gospel in the whole world; and its very universalism, its members believed, guaranteed it against error: *securus iudicat orbis terrarum.*

Of course it was an unrealised and unrealisable ideal; a glance at church history should make that clear enough. Nevertheless the fact that an ideal is unrealised or even unrealisable within the course of history does not invalidate it. The nature of the church, its holiness and its unity as much as its Catholicity, is something to be striven for, something hoped for in God's future, at least as much as it is something ever actually realised in any particular space–time context. Yet we can see that it has been more realised in one context than another – much more, for instance, in a context of the early centuries which was able to accept Greek, Latin, Armenian, Syrian and Copt, all as equally first-class citizens, than in a later age which largely restricted Catholicism to modes of Christian expression characteristic of a single culture. But the exclusions of whole groups of Christians consequent upon the narrowing down of pluralism claimed justification not as such in cultural terms but in those of the failure of one or another tradition of doctrinal expression to be adequately faithful to the original revelation, that which had to be expressed. All agreed that in principle such exclusions could be necessary but all, or almost all, failed to realise how inevitable it was that in the course of history and the diversity of language the ceaseless cultural reinterpretation, linguistic and philosophical retranslation, of the original vision would not be identical with, but only to a greater or lesser extent equivalent within a new context to, the original gospel 'once delivered to the Saints'.

One might say that before the nineteenth-century, before Newman began the attempt to make explicit the intrinsic process of change he labelled 'development' and defended as justifiable and indeed inevitable, the only proof that the tradition is actually alive, Christians were so deeply unaware of the internal dialectic within their tradition that they were more or less compelled to belittle or even condemn as heretical a great part of its contemporary expression in favour of some imaginary, and fundamentalistic, past pattern of Catholic wholeness or of biblical and apostolic purity.

Catholicism came thus to have a double meaning, though the duality was unrecognised. On the one hand a wholeness, theologically only possible in a hoped for but unimaginable future kingdom, but held, with greater or less historic justification, to have existed in some golden age of church history, such as the apostolic era or the time of the Council of Nicaea; on the other, the actual, limited form which contemporary Christianity had come to take in a later age and a particular ecclesio-cultural tradition. This was most obviously the case for the Latin West, medieval and post-medieval, the tradition in fact most committed to the nominal use of the word and in consequence that which has ever since come to be in practice defined by the name of Catholic, the communion of Rome. Catholicism has here come to mean a pattern of Christian faith and practice stressing sacraments, hierarchy, religious orders, the value of celibacy, the dominance of scholastic theology and canon law, above all the decisive authority of the See of Rome. Catholicism in this sense means a form of Christianity stabilised in a rather rigid way in the Latin West between the eleventh and the thirteenth centuries and maintained substantially unchanged from then until the twentieth century within the Roman Catholic Church.

The high point of its formulation was at the First Vatican Council of 1870. While there almost always remained some recognition that Catholicism does not need to be totally Roman and neo-scholastic, a recognition that liturgical languages and rites other than the Latin could exist, that a more biblical or patristic theology was not necessarily heretical, nevertheless in practice for centuries Catholicism accorded only rather second-class citizenship to anyone deviating significantly from the Latin and scholastic model. The continual tendency from the reign of Gregory VII to that of Pius XII was a progressive normalisation and centralisation of Catholicism in terms of current Roman practice.

The model of Catholicism which prevailed throughout those centuries and in which my own generation was still brought up was, then, unquestionably monolithic and precise. It was anything but pluralist, either socially or theologically. It justified the use of Latin throughout the liturgy, it entirely excluded the laity and all nuns from communion of the cup, it insisted upon the celibacy of the clergy, it at least theoretically justified discrimination against non-Catholics in Catholic countries. It had never begun to repudiate the Inquisition, Roman or Spanish, and where possible, as through concordats with Mussolini or Salazar, it still obtained whatever political privileges it could to place it above any other religious group. The devotion to Isabella of Castile, 'La Catolica', has prevailed into the twentieth century. She is still proposed as a candidate for canonisation and she still represents almost normatively what could – at least until thirty years ago – be reasonably regarded as a true face of Catholicism. She and her husband were, *par excellence* and by papal nomination, 'the Catholic sovereigns'. They had earned the title by their zeal in promoting the Inquisition and by expelling all Moslems and Jews from Spain in 1492. In 1992 we might have done well to remember less the discovery of America by Columbus than the lamentably disgraceful expulsion of the Jews from a country they had come to see almost as their second chosen land. It was an action in line with the increasing religious intolerance of the later Middle Ages but also deeply determinative of the character of Catholicism for centuries to come. While Jews continued to reside in some other Catholic countries, nowhere did they do so with the increasing freedom of those in Protestant countries such as Holland and England, or in the Balkans under the Ottoman Empire. Here indeed we are looking at the narrowest of Catholic models, but still one in close organic relationship with its central ongoing form.

Protestantism was, in origin, exactly what the word suggests – a movement of protest against the dominant existing model, that is to say late medieval, papally controlled, Catholicism. Led by priests and monks, it was certainly not an attack on Catholicism in our first sense, but an attempt to recover it as against the deformations of Catholicism in our second sense. If Catholicism is understood as the pursuit of an unchanging ideal through changing forms, the character of a pilgrim people through history, then it should certainly be perceived as requiring oscillations of protest and reform if it is to retain an underlying fidelity to the faith and ideals of its origins: *Ecclesia semper reformanda*, an old adage which Congar brought back to our consciousness.

Protestantism, then, can be seen as an example of a mechanism within the very structure of Catholicism requisite for the historical retention of its balance and purity. That is not at all to say that everything the Protestant reformers of the sixteenth century said, all the attacks they made on current Catholic belief and practice, were necessarily right. They were not after all agreed among themselves, and why should they be? What was valid as part of a healthy Catholicism was Protestantism as a movement of sincere, scripture-grounded critique and reform made at a time when the church was undoubtedly in a pretty shabby state. It has absolutely to be seen as in purpose part of the organic life of the Catholic whole, not a breaking apart to form some other whole. There can be in the end but one Christian whole: that was common ground to all sides in the separations of the sixteenth century. But the Catholicism of the time, more papally dominated than ever after the collapse of the conciliar movement, could not conceive of such a movement as justifiable. There were of course significant bridge personalities, Catholic reformers who had much in common with their Protestant contemporaries. But by and large the Roman and Catholic reaction was to reject and to condemn and in this there was only too much in common with the attitude of many of the reformers. A slanging match in the coarsest language constituted too much of sixteenth-century religious dialogue.

The result of the process was the hardening of two restricted systems, Catholicism and Protestantism, though the latter at least was never intended to become such. The early Protestants did not want to create Protestantism; they wanted to reform Catholicism. Protestantism, as we know it in its various forms, grew out of the ecclesial vacuum created by the rejection of Roman imperialism by reformers and monarchs and the necessity of developing one or another ecclesiastical and doctrinal system to take its place, often in reality a depressingly erastian system. Despite variations it shared a common rejection of large elements of standard late medieval Catholicism. Thus it everywhere insisted upon the vernacular Bible and its availability to the laity, vernacular services, lay communion of the cup, a married, or at least marriageable, clergy.

Behind all this lay a theology of faith and grace which may well be contrasted sharply enough with the theology informing the late-medieval piety of multiple masses for the dead, indulgences, pilgrimages, relics and the rest. It is, however, arguable that the theologies of faith and grace of Reformation and Counter-Reformation were by no means irreconcilable, or, at least, that one moderately tolerant church could have contained all the main ones. What was irreconcilable was Protestant insistence upon a number of important and necessary reforms in worship and ministry, of freedom to maintain and develop a range of theological opinions, with the Roman refusal to allow space for such reforms and theological views. Rome admitted no possibility of appeal beyond the voice of the living church, in practice beyond itself. Protestantism insisted upon the validity of just such an appeal – to scripture, the Spirit, conscience or reason – but found it very hard to formulate a satisfactory way of handling that appeal in the present.

It is impossible not to recognise the clear contrast between what historically from the sixteenth to the mid-twentieth century existed as two separate and rival systems. Of course, they shared much: the Nicene Creed, the scriptures, the authority of the Fathers, the doctrines of the Trinity, the Incarnation, the Redemption and a great deal more. But in terms of 95 per cent of their members, this shared foundation was mediated through highly contrasting systems, each of which had to be defended against the other. Papal authority, Latin, celibate priests, lots of monks and nuns, indulgences, canonisations, relics and pilgrimages upon the one hand; an omnipresence of the Bible, church authority never wider than national, everything in the vernacular, universal communion of the cup, a highly monogamous clergy, upon the other.

The edges on both sides were undoubtedly frayed. There were some liberal Catholics who wished at least to stop papal authority growing ever larger, there were some Protestants who, especially in England but also elsewhere, wanted to regain lost elements within the Catholic package. Once the Tractarian movement and Anglo-Catholicism had begun to affect the Church of England, our binary model became seriously confused. It is a reason why for ordinary English members of the national church, quite convinced that they were Protestant, Anglo-Catholicism could be so absurdly unpopular. It failed to fit within the categories, but it also finally failed to disrupt them.

The picture I am presenting here is a sociological portrayal of Christianity as much as a theological one, and it does not as such imply an evaluation of either side. However it would be manifestly mistaken to think that either of these alternative systems was wholly right in the things in which it contrasted with the other. Without going exhaustively into this, I would for instance judge Catholicism profoundly right in finding room for and valuing the celibate, in its greater concern with the mystical and the symbolic, in its willingness to add to what is explicit in scripture particularly through a greater openness to other religious traditions, artistic inspiration and the practices of popular piety.

Fifty years ago a Catholic would have been in considerable trouble for suggesting that over any serious matter Protestants had been right and Rome wrong. Today, even on explicitly Catholic principles, I don't think that it is possible to deny this. The acceptance by the Second Vatican Council and Paul VI in the immediately post-conciliar years of a vernacular liturgy, lay admission to communion of the cup, the practice of concelebration which soon brought an end to the liturgical scandal of simultaneous 'private' masses said on a multitude of adjacent altars, all involved the belated acceptance of major points of Reformation criticism. No less significant were the Constitution on Revelation, sanctioning a real pastoral revolution in attitudes to scripture, and the Declaration on Religious Freedom. On these and other matters the highest authority within Catholicism decisively rejected segments of the post-Reformation Catholic synthesis and adopted what were in fact segments of the Protestant synthesis.

In making these quite revolutionary decisions the Council and Pope Paul doubtless did not see themselves as Protestantising, though they did most certainly see themselves as establishing a new ground on which to relate to Protestantism. Probably few of the Council Fathers or even the Council *Periti* realised how far they were going, materially, in a Protestant direction. What was happening was a redefinition of the ideal of Catholicism, less in substantively medieval terms and more in those of an earlier model – a model which Protestants could to a greater extent share. By accepting the objective validity of part of the Reformation critique of late medieval Catholicism, the Council was nevertheless puncturing a good part of the binary model I have been sketching. For many Christians the difference between Catholicism and Protestantism would no longer be very clear. It would become quite easy to cross and recross the divide, and joint ecumenical services were encouraging more and more people to do so. Two generations ago very few people would even have called themselves Christians: they were Baptists, Presbyterians, Anglicans, above all they were Protestants or Roman Catholics. Today the name of Christian has returned to regular usage and many a believer would object to being precisely defined as anything more than that.

If this sea-change in attitudes was prepared for by the Ecumenical Movement over a number of decades, it was the Vatican Council which, by quite suddenly involving Roman Catholics within it, forced almost everyone else as well to a profound reconsideration of where they stood in regard to Catholicism. Perhaps it was the presence of observers from other churches at all four sessions of the Council and the close co-operation which this produced that psychologically ended the sense of two contrasting communities and recreated an awareness of substantial, if incomplete, unity. The observers helped the Council enormously and modern Catholicism increasingly recognised its profound wider indebtedness to modern Protestantism – for biblical translations, historical scholarship and a commonsense approval of modern democratic society. At the same time and in part in consequence of the Catholic conversion – for what happened at Vatican II was no less than a conversion – Protestants found their eyes reopened to the strengths, liturgical, organisational and spiritual, of modern Catholicism. The 1960s and 1970s were as a result decades of amazing cross-fertilisation, represented by such documents as the ARCIC agreements but by vastly much more than that. The Christian theological world today is totally inexplicable without this near fusion of what before 1960 were almost segregated thought-circles. There is simply no way in which we could return to that segregation. The middle wall of partition has been removed, intellectually and spiritually if not institutionally, and few of us are not profoundly grateful that this is so.

Nevertheless strictly speaking Vatican II formally authorised no such desegregation. The adoption of many important propositions hitherto part of the Protestant and not the Catholic package did not in theory dismantle the latter. John Huss had always been judged an heretic, a proto-Protestant ever since he died in the fire of the Council of Constance in 1415. Now it could be blithely declared that this was a mistake. The Reformist policies he died for could be incorporated in a somewhat enlarged Catholicism, communion in both kinds could be adopted, but – despite the appearance of a return to what one might call a first millennium model of Catholic Christianity, incompatible with the Catholic package as a whole in the post-Tridentine period – the controlling principle of Catholicism as it had emerged in the West in the period from the Gregorian Reform was not in fact discarded. It was the principle which finally produced the schism of the Reformation, just as it had produced the schism with the Greek East. That principle was the total ecclesiastical authority of the See of Rome. Other elements in the traditional Catholic package could be discarded as outworn, but this – the one and only absolutely decisive one – has not been. It very nearly was in the context of the discussion of collegiality, in the course of which an essentially different model of ecclesial authority came once more to the Catholic surface, reminding one of the conciliarist debates of the fifteenth century and necessarily relativising papal supremacy. The Council emphatically affirmed a collegial model in chapter 3 of *Lumen Gentium*, but it was over-careful, under Pope Paul's directions, to insist that this in no way subtracted from the essentially supremacist model which Catholicism had worked with for centuries, and, while it was silent about the word 'monarchy' – hitherto so much favoured in Roman theology – it produced no collegial machinery to replace the monarchical machinery of power long in place.

In the post-conciliar euphoria common to Catholic and Protestant alike and in the earlier years of ecumenical dialogue which followed, this crucial point was not sufficiently noted. So much had changed that it was not realised that the essential principle of division between Catholic and Protestant or – perhaps – Roman Catholics and all other Christians had not. The binary divide in theory remained, yet the changes which had taken place had undermined its plausibility. In fact it remained in the minds of the pope, the Roman Curia, a certain number of bishops and the code of Canon Law, but it could hardly be said to remain in the collective commitment of Catholic theologians, the pastoral clergy or the more diffused consciousness of large parts of the laity. They had all understood that the logic of Vatican II went beyond its letter, that collegiality needed to be made into a reality rather than minimalised and that it needed as soon as possible to be seen as embracing, rather than excluding, the bishops of the Orthodox and other churches.

Thirty years since the start of the Council we have now reached a position in which we can, painfully if realistically, map out the current relationship between Catholicism and Protestantism once more. The great tide powered by Vatican II has, at least institutionally, spent its force. The old landscape has once more emerged and Vatican II is now being read in Rome far more in the spirit of Vatican I and within the context of Pius XII's model of Catholicism. That is the basic institutional fact with which we have all to reckon in the pontificate of John Paul II. However the very clarity of current Roman policy may have helped many Catholics to see that Vatican II can be better read as an imperfectly expressed attempt to revive the very different ecclesiology of concilia-rism, to accept the very core of the Reformation critique, and to recognise that the late medieval Catholic system, carried through five centuries and across Vatican I to reach its high point in the reign of Pius XII, was in considerable measure unCatholic, unChristian and untenable. To hold the latter view in no way means to reject the papacy or the kind of role it played in the first five centuries of the church, but it does mean to reject a monarchical papacy of the sort already rejected by the Orthodox in the East and Protestants in the West. It almost certainly means rejecting the ecumenicity of Vatican I, something which almost no Catholic theologian would have dared to suggest thirty years ago, but which many today take almost for granted.

It is very clear then what the stakes are in the almost titanic conflict now developing within the Catholic Church. On one side the model of Catholicism as described earlier remains essentially unchanged: a mono-lithic church wholly dependent upon its central Roman authority and in which the bishops have actually less freedom than they had in pre-Vatican II days, a church ministered to and controlled by an all-male, celibate clergy, seemingly preoccupied with Marian devotion and the canon-isation of new saints. Never indeed have so many saints been canonised as in the pontificate of John Paul II. In comparison with the essential stability of the model, the points that have changed, such as the liturgical use of the vernacular, can seem fairly small. The system, at its core a matter of authority and of power, has not. It is the same system against which Luther protested in the sixteenth century.

Against this model a great many Catholics now propose an alterna-tive. Collegiality was affirmed, they say, but it was not applied. It cannot be applied while bishops are all appointed and controlled by Rome; that is not conducive to a college. Against the monism of an infallible papacy, a model demonstrated historically to be fallacious, they suggest a pluralism of collegial episcopate and council, papacy and laity, the guidance of the Spirit and the abiding norm of the scriptures. It is a model which undoubtedly fails to provide an infallible mechanism available at any precise time and is open to all the problems which Protestants have experienced in the past in attempting to locate authority, nevertheless it is a model consonant with human society and ecclesiastical history and one whose ultimate viability can be seen as dependent not upon a rule of thumb but upon faith in the presence of God's Spirit in the church.

For centuries there has not been such a large and profound

theological debate within the Catholic Church. In some ways Rome's increasingly systematic attempt to crush alternative theologies reminds one of the suppression of modernism at the beginning of the century in the pontificate of Pius X. But the theology it would now like to suppress has a far better *droit de cité* within Catholicism than had modernism at that time, it is also more widely spread and for a large part in theological institutions – such as most of the Catholic universities of the USA – which are no longer effectively under Roman control. While the bishops may be dragooned into line, externally at least (and it must be remembered that an increasingly high proportion have been selected in the pontificate of John Paul II), theologians cannot be to anything like the same extent, though their status as *Catholic* theologians can be, and in some cases has been, denied.

In this struggle, the whole nature of Catholicism is in question. Is it to remain something with which Protestantism has still to be contrasted, or is it to become again, across an extension of the logic of Vatican II, something to which classical Protestantism sees itself as belonging in the way the Reformers once wished to belong? Christians in other churches have in this predicament to decide how they understand their ecumenical task in relation to Roman Catholicism and there are fundamentally two different ways in which they can do so. The first is to accept that the nature of Roman Catholicism is appropriately defined by the current, canonically valid, Roman leadership. It is not for Protestants to challenge that definition but to attempt to maintain good relations with its makers by a cautious, polite dialogue which accepts that Rome is Rome and Protestantism is Protestantism, and never the two shall meet. It would be the way of HM Government relating to any well-established tyrant the world over. The second is to insist that Catholics and Protestants are not two sorts of being but rather two groups of one sort of being, a Christian being. If Rome's insistence on its own monolithic control of the church, on the law of clerical celibacy and so on, would be intolerable for Protestants for themselves, then it should remain intolerable for Catholics today too. And Protestants, Anglicans or whatever, should continually make it clear that they believe this to be so. It is not ecumenically desirable that they should forever muffle their voice in order not to displease their official partners in dialogue. We are not a different species of Christian. See in us rather a mirror of the Reformation. Catholics in communion with Rome are endeavouring to do today what Luther and others were endeavouring, but in a way failed, to do four hundred years ago: to free the large central communion of Christendom from a medieval incubus of power concentration, sexual inhibitions and phoney devotions in order to allow the great stream of Christian faith, hope and love flowing forth from cross and gospel, scripture and early apostolic experience to find its own way within the pluralism of our human world.

Catholicism and Protestantism may still remain as two attitudes of mind, the one concerned with guarding the *status quo*, the accumulations of history as they are gathered, canonically and intellectually, into one or another attempted new synthesis and upheld by the authority of the church of the present, the other concerned with a critique of the perennial failure of the present to be faithful to the wholeness of the original vision, the demands of scripture, of truth, of the revolutionary requirements of the Spirit of Jesus in every age. In this sense we will always need both Catholics and Protestants but we need them within a single communion and one not structured so as to place the boot too firmly upon one foot alone.

It would be disastrous if Protestants now turned away from Roman Catholicism with nothing but bitterness that the springtime of Vatican II had turned back to storm and disillusionment, but it would be little less disastrous if they wiped the tears from their eyes and settled for a never ending polite dialogue with an unchanging infallibilist Rome. The reaction of the present pontificate cannot continue; it is simply not re-establishing a functional system. The post-Tridentine Roman Catholicism of the past cannot return except in a pathetically shrunken form any more than the stable Protestantisms of the Post-Reformation era can return. We are all being shaken to pieces by the intellectual and moral storms of the late twentieth century. Vatican II was far more than an attempt to overcome the blockage of the post-Reformation agenda; it was, still more, an attempt to grapple with the new agendas of our time: infinitely more difficult but still more necessary if Christianity, Catholic or Protestant, is to survive, to flourish, to carry on a message of meaning, of hope, of a sanity not human but divine, to a world of the twenty-first century threatened in its very existence as the world never has been threatened until our age. To do that we need both temperamental Catholics and temperamental Protestants, wrestling within a single communion; we need the inheritance of Huss and Luther, just as we need a papacy liberated from its imperialist hallucinations and free to be genuinely a 'see of unity'. Those of us who remain within the communion of Rome, realising that we are Protestants but still ones who cannot bear to cease to be Catholics, can only appeal to our fellow Protestants of other communions to hope and pray that, through the drama of post–Vatican II Catholicism, the middle wall of partition which has divided us since the sixteenth century may indeed be finally broken down and the unity of the Body of Christ, one, holy Church of God, be visibly recovered.

Lenten Lecture, Centre for Reformation Studies, University of Sheffield, 8 April 1992

Prophecy
Today

9

Church and State in a Pluralist Society

'We are finding ourselves disestablished almost everywhere except in the lunatic asylums.' Bishop Gore's often quoted remark made in a speech in the House of Lords in 1913 was not part of a plea for formal disestablishment but one for recognition of the fact that in reality disestablishment had already taken place: the pluralism of British society had required the steady diminution of establishment throughout the course of the previous hundred years to a level that would have seemed hardly imaginable in the age of Keble's sermon on National Apostasy. Moreover, creeping disestablishment has gone a great deal further since 1913. It was inevitable that it should, but in consequence we need to recognise that the issue has ceased to be a genuinely significant one. The central case against establishment as it once was is that it effectively eliminates the freedom of the church to stand apart from political power, free to proclaim a message uncongenial to Caesar. Equally it inherently discriminates against citizens who are non-members of the church. The critical distance required between church and state disappears. It did so in post-Henrician England, just as it did in the papal states or in the Byzantine empire of Justinian.

The point of making Gore's pungent remark our starting point, however, is also to suggest the almost endless historical diversity to be found in church–state relations, even when papered over by the continued simple use of some single term such as 'establishment'. It has been used to refer to so many different patterns of relationship. Some years ago I produced for a seminar at the School of Oriental and African Studies a typology of church–state relations in which I listed a lengthy series of relevant ecclesiastical and political factors producing different types of relationship, and I labelled my series with letters from A to Z. In the seminar Professor Roland Oliver asked somewhat incredulously whether these were really all the characteristics and varieties conceivable, or whether I had stopped where I did because, reaching the letter Z, I had no more labels to make use of. I said it was the first, but now I rather doubt it; the diversification possible could hardly be adequately treated with a mere twenty-six letters of the alphabet. I believe that, given such diversity, discussion as to what is appropriate in the field of church–state relations can only be helpful if it is very carefully contextualised historically. How usable is the British tradition of church–state relations in terms of the new Europe?

High Anglican theory underlying the substantial identity of church and national society was best formulated by Hooker. It implied a symbiosis in which church and state each profoundly took on characteristics impressed upon it by the other, and that was indeed Tudor reality – up to a point. Beautifully formulated, it has continued to bewitch, even in the twentieth century. I suppose it bewitched William Temple to some degree and T. S. Eliot too. It may be best seen as essentially a theory of social science, and theories of social science are seldom more than somewhat rough approximations to the infinite complexity of human social existence. It never fully worked, but it did function sufficiently well, in the eyes of its beneficiaries at least, not to fall into obvious desuetude for a very long while and, unlike some theories of social science, it provided at its best a high moral philosophy for the state, a public doctrine upon which people could fall back with confidence, neither pure theology nor pure political theory but an artful composite of both.

In the onward march of historical reality the post-Reformation relationship of church and state in England was, however, always more complicated, more pragmatic, more a matter of piously cloaking naked power; and it never stayed still for long. The history of establishment is the history of a score or so of different ways in which English Christianity has both influenced and been controlled by English society and political authority. Hookerian theory in part reflected reality but in part it was just a dream, ignoring both the sheer secularity of the state and the dogged obstinacy with which significant religious minorities of the English nation refused to be included. There was always, in consequence, an alternative non-Anglican, non-establishment history of church–state relations in this country. The nation's final inability, at the dawn of a more liberal age, to deny first-class citizenship to Roman Catholics and

Free Churchmen publicly undermined, in the course of the nineteenth century, the social foundation of Anglican establishment. Anything after that was just a mopping-up operation. Establishment had implied that only one church–state relationship existed or mattered. Instead there were several. Cabinet ministers had to listen to Free Church leaders – Lloyd George inviting them to breakfast time 'love feasts' in Number 10 – as also to the Cardinal Archbishop of Westminster and to many other Cardinal Archbishops around the Empire. This could only diminish the political standing of Anglican bishops from one point of view, though it actually enhanced it from another. If Cardinal Manning could intervene in a strike, the Bishop of Durham might do so too. In this altered, more plural context, it was easier to rediscover the values and the advantages of a greater freedom of action. Nor did the admission of pluralism necessarily preclude a larger, less structured, unity in Christianity's public voice in circumstances when it really mattered. The letter to *The Times* of 21 December 1940 signed by Archbishops Lang and Temple, Cardinal Hinsley and the Moderator of the Free Church Federal Council on the Pope's Five Peace Points was, doubtless, only the proverbial first swallow, but it still hinted at the possibility that, beyond establishment, a unitary ecclesial voice might on occasion be obtainable.

The point of all this is to suggest that, in fact, and without any sudden emphatic or ideologically-constructed change of law, England moved gently and rather beneficially to a pattern of the relationship of church and state far more complex and less easily formulated than that of establishment.

The state of which we are citizens is not, however, England, frequently as Englishmen have been inclined to forget it. We have for several centuries been citizens, instead, of a united kingdom, a union but not a fusion of nations. Perhaps the most obvious weakness within the ideology of Anglican establishment, at least since the Act of Union in 1707 and even more since that of 1800, has been failure to recognise the ecclesiastical implication of these acts; but this has only been part of a far wider English failure to think through the inherent difference between England and Britain, the part and the whole. The Church of England remained the Church of England, unestablished in Scotland, yet subject – as royal supremacy turned into parliamentary supremacy – to a body now in principle British, not English, the sovereign assembly for regions in which the form of Christianity we could define as Anglican was actually not only not established but for a while proscribed. Normative

Anglican thinking remained bewitched by the unanalysed mirage of a triangle consisting of nation-state, national church, established church.

The much-admired Max Warren was General Secretary of the Church Missionary Society for twenty years during the 1940s and 1950s, a period of decisive transformation of the church in the non-Western world. He had become an outstanding missionary statesman and ecclesiastical sage, before retiring to a canonry at Westminster. I remember with much pleasure visiting him there. His world-wide missionary responsibilities had led him to ponder the subject of church–state relations a great deal and he wrote widely about them, including *Caesar, the Beloved Enemy*, a nice title and one of which he was rather fond, but the force of which, I suspect, may still have eluded him. The tension within Max between mid-twentieth century international statesman and old-fashioned Anglican Evangelical never quite surfaced in so equable a man. In Advent 1963 he gave three lectures in Westminster Abbey on *The Functions of a National Church*. They were printed at the time and have recently been reprinted. I have to confess that I found reading them a rather disappointing experience. Reflecting upon it, I would locate the reason in Max's inability to be critical about the concept of a nation and, still more, a nation state. 'A nation is an entity in its own right,' he declared, adding that in 'a Biblical understanding of history, nations are part of a providential ordering of human life.' Again, 'By the State I mean the Society of a Nation viewed as an organisation for the preservation and good ordering of the life of the Nation' (17). 'The National Church of this country', he argued, has 'a real ministry' towards 'purifying the imagination of the State in regard to the exercise of power' (26).

Some of these statements appear uncomfortably close to the Christian nationalism of the main line of Dutch Reformed Afrikaner thinking in South Africa, and that should at once make one pause; but if we confine our reflections for a while to this country, we need to remind ourselves that the state in which we live is not a national state and has never had, since the eighteenth century, a single national state church. The Scots and the English are not a single nation and never have been, let alone the Irish and the Welsh. The basic mistake here is not an ecclesiastical or a theological one, but sociological and political. Our state, like most other states, has not been – in Warren's phrase – 'the society of a nation'. The unanalysed assumption that this was the case has all along been profoundly damaging to the identity of minorities within the state – the smaller nations of which it consists, and of the smaller churches.

Anglicans are simply too important in our present and our future to be allowed, without remonstrance, to continue with such sloppy thinking, even when sanctioned – alas – by one as wise as Max Warren. Yet his lectures were reprinted in the 1980s as representing the acme of wisdom upon church and state. If the model of the nation state has been a disastrous model for western Europe and one of its most unfortunate of exports, then its baneful influence has also to be detected at home and in its appendage, the national church or – far worse – the state church. Yet beneath the verbiage our reality in this country has long been different, more creative, more pluralist, more profoundly biblical.

Analysis of the reality of the United Kingdom only reinforces the analysis already made of the modern religious state of England alone. Each is and has long been one of pluralism. The reality of our British experience has been that, despite monopolistic dreams, we have steadily struggled from positions both within and without the established churches to escape from the singularity of a definable church–state relationship. And this is the case, not only at the level of a multiplicity of distinct churches, but also at the level of organisations, groups and individuals. Within the very heart of establishment, for example, the history of the Church Missionary Society in reality involved a profound erosion of the mechanics of establishment by developing a very influential area of church life unaffected by crown appointment: probably no twentieth-century Anglican, unappointed to his position by the crown, was so ecclesiastically influential as Max Warren when General Secretary of the CMS. Today Christian Aid, the Catholic Institute of International Relations, and many other bodies and individuals from Frank Field to the Bishop of Oxford, all represent differing faces of the church *vis à vis* the state and public political life. The model of establishment, most especially in its English form, was one of an essentially single relationship between church and state, a relationship defined by the latter. The more plural the relationship, the less it can be state-controlled or establishmentarian, but also of course the less it is defined either by a single monolithic church.

It is noteworthy that Max Warren, having spelt out the actual functions needed of a national church very sanely, found himself concluding 'The threefold vocation which I have attempted to outline ... is, I believe, the vocation of every church, even the smallest minority in the most unfavourable environment' (34). In other words such functions have actually nothing to do with this theologically phoney category 'the

National Church'. Every church has a duty to 'purify the imagination of the State in regard to the exercise of power', though, admittedly, if you take that function seriously, it may at times be easier to do something effectively about it if you live in a Westminster canonry beside the Houses of Parliament. But one has to do it from many another vantage point, including a theological chair in a civic university.

It may be seen as an accident of history but it is also intrinsic to the character of modern Britain that our Christianity has developed so pluralistically – far more so than that of any other European country. If this is so, it is because British Christians have awkwardly insisted upon making it so, obstinately refusing in all sorts of ways and despite all sorts of penalties to accept the principle *cujus regio ejus et religio*. They preferred to suffer in Bedford Gaol, on the gallows at Tyburn or York or in the fires of Smithfield. Instead of seeing ourselves as heirs to either Thomas More or Thomas Cranmer, we need to think of ourselves as in fact we are, the heirs of both. Perhaps neither wanted pluralism and each would have given to the state more than we would give, but it was the hard determination of Christians of different persuasions to resist the State's *diktat* which collectively constructed our pluralism, and it is this pluralism far more than establishment which provides the heart of our church–state experience in this country.

It remains, nevertheless, a very exciting thing about the pluralisation of the British religious scene that it was achieved without its privatisation. The minorities had to fight the establishment for their just rights both as Christians and as citizens, and for the intrinsic freedom of the church itself in its public role, but they managed to do it and win the battle without actually demolishing the establishment or inducing the state to withdraw into a position of religious indifference. Hence Charles Gore's complaint – we have been disestablished everywhere except in the lunatic asylums. It was not, of course, quite true or he would not have been there to deliver a speech in the House of Lords. To the Lords and the lunatics one could add the prisons, the coronation of the Sovereign and much else. Not too insignificant a list. The point is that while the survival of the formality of establishment has ceased seriously to threaten the freedom of the church or its ability to call the tune in its relationship with the state, establishment is still there to assert constitutionally, publicly and symbolically the church's relevance both to public policy and to the care of the most needy, in prison, mental hospitals, or wherever.

Good as such a survival is, it would not be acceptable in our highly pluralistic society, if it were still to be treated as a narrowly Anglican matter. Legally that is the case in reality; I trust that it is now recognised not to be. The bishops in the House of Lords cannot really be there as Anglicans but rather as representatives of the Spirituality, a voice of Christianity and of religion even wider than Christianity. Maybe they do not do it perfectly and it is certainly something of a chore for busy men. But it remains in principle right, even wonderful, that it should be done and a part of our constitution. It would be a sad day if either a Labour government or a more fundamentalist church swept it away in the interests of the supposed separation of the religious from the political or of some rather boring secular formula deemed appropriate for elections to second chambers. But what most matters in all this is that the idea that religion is a mere private matter for modern society (easily implied in formal disestablishment) has been avoided and the tradition of the church's public responsibility maintained.

Our progressive pluralisation has then proved compatible with a reduced but still meaningful establishment and beneficially so. Now it is that package of pluralism and establishment, each giving support to the other, which is about the most valuable thing we can take with us into Europe in the 1990s. It has borne many good fruits in the United Kingdom in the sensible co-operation it has made possible in all sorts of areas of life, especially the educational. We must now, I believe, try to make this sort of approach operational within the wider forum of a federal Europe.

The pluralism we possess and which I seem to have been praising a good deal may seem to some a defect rather than an asset or a virtue. Is it not just a consequence of fragmentation, of the dissolution of past unity? Should not the church be one rather than plural? Is not any degree of self-congratulation upon something which can be seen precisely as a fruit of Christian disagreements essentially misplaced? Undoubtedly the Ecumenical Movement was the most important thing that happened to the Christian world in the last generation and a simple application of ecumenical logic might easily be thought to require the answering of a 'Yes' to all such questions. It would all the same be a poor answer because one unable to cope in a sophisticated way with either the complexities of our actual historical situation or the inherent complexities of Christian faith. Truth has always to be a primary concern and requires that we start from a recognition of social, intellectual and spiritual reality. Christian reality has grown so pluriform, and that pluriformity is so clearly rooted in the very nature and flexibility of the tradition from its start – rather than in some latter-day aberration – that we need to accept a very substantial validity to our pluriformity, only moving on from there to realise the ecclesial qualities of unity, catholicity, apostolicity and holiness.

We should count ourselves profoundly fortunate that we have within our English tradition both Catholic and Protestant versions of the Christian totality represented so positively and, indeed, so ecumenically. The Eastern Orthodox version too is now quite effectively rooted in this country. It is also a simple fact that it is only when people start from a recognition of pluriformity that they do actually move a bit nearer to unity, while the assertion of the necessity of any one formulated model of unity – even some recently concocted ecumenical model – all too easily bars the way. Pluralism, moreover, is particularly necessary and useful in relation to the political field because it does a great deal to inhibit one of the most frequent failings of public Christianity: the transformation of Christian influence into a matter of power politics, heavy handling by a religious big brother.

To summarise my argument: the pluralism of the British Christian tradition is, and has long been, an accepted and thoroughly fruitful fact, even if hidden just a bit by a facile concentration upon the far more easily identifiable issue of a surviving establishment. What I am suggesting is that we have handled it pragmatically but rather well, in part precisely because we did not push the anti-establishment case right through, and that it provides in consequence a very considerable resource to offer the new Europe, a resource which would simply cease to exist if we returned to harping instead on the pros and cons of establishment. Many of the churches of Europe remain in reality a good deal more established in any particular place or country than anything you could find in Britain outside the most Presbyterian areas of Scotland. Almost every area of the continent remains far more tied to, and characterised by, its local history of Reformation and Counter-Reformation, with Roman Catholic dominance in one place, some form of national Protestant church in another. We have had a far more diversified religious history in the eighteenth, nineteenth and even twentieth century than is to be found elsewhere. In eastern Europe, moreover, we see only too well, with the collapse of Communism, the danger of a falling-back into the most simplistic of national religious identifications: Catholic Croats, Orthodox Serbs, Muslim Albanians. None of that is wholly true, but the degree of identification is sufficient for the appeal of small national states, backed by their particular form of national religion, to be intensely dangerous both for society and for religion. The attraction of a pathetically narrow nationalism, feeding on and debasing religion, has been manifest in the Ukraine, in Lithuania, in Rumania, in the revived anti-semitism of Catholic Austria, just as on both sides in Northern Ireland. Not the legal structures of establishment maybe, but the psychology, the pathology of nationalism, a national church and a nation state, are very much there in many places, threatening both European peace and Christian wisdom.

If Europe is to grow into a tolerant, co-operative harmony – and quite the same is true of Africa and of Asia – then the structures and borders of political, national and religious communities need to be differentiated rather than identified. The political community is something larger than the national, tribal community, and the religious community is something quite different from either, and something which may only be able to fulfil the sort of functions which Max Warren indicated to be those of a church *vis à vis* a state, if it can be clearly seen not to be a national church in any very strong sense. In a formal sense the national church was a fruit of the Reformation, one of its more dubious fruits, twin to the national state. Today we have to pass beyond both one and the other, but we will be able to do so only to the degree that we can establish a pluriformity of loyalties and of communities.

I have talked so far as if, while the church was pluralist, the political community was unitary. Only with the Isle of Man and the Channel Islands did we tolerate pluralism, because we thought them unimportant. These apart, we feared to dilute the sovereignty of Westminster. Yet the whole concept of a single location of sovereignty – for long the one *de fide* article of the British Constitution – can be a dangerous and deceptive one. Should we retain our sovereignty? Have we lost it already to Brussels? It is only too clear that one of the most outspoken and clear-minded protagonists of the sovereignty school, Enoch Powell, is also one of the most emphatic apologists for a national, established church, subservient to Parliament. That is in itself revealing. The mistake has been the location of sovereignty in a single person or institution, comparable to the location of ecclesiastical power in a single person, the *plena potestas* of the pope. It is far better to think of sovereignty, power, authority, as being rightfully diffused by their very essence, realisable only collegially and in a range of ways across an inherent separation of powers. We hope that the Europe we are moving towards will not be one in which sovereignty is monopolised anew by a dictatorial and bureaucratic Brussels, but a revived medieval *communitas communitatum* within which it is shared and balanced so that, in a way, no one can say where it is. Henry VIII may well be seen as the originator of the myth of a simple national sovereignty as well as of a national erastian church. Having grown beyond the one, we should not be surprised to be getting beyond the other too.

If the danger is to get beyond a national state into a monolithically regulated west European state, the comparable ecclesiastical danger would be to succumb once more to a uniform international church. That may not seem too grave a threat. In religious terms, however, western Europe is predominantly Catholic and the Catholic Church is now being so disciplined in a new Ultramontanism that it is conceivable that in the sphere of organised religion Brussels might relate quite closely to the papacy and to very little else. It is crucial to the health of the public Christian role in the new Europe that it should not appear limited to a papalist Catholicism on the one hand and a few rather nationally-circum-scribed Protestant churches on the other. The religious input, the dialogue between church and state, needs to be able to cross the Catholic–Protestant line a great deal more easily and fluently than that, to be pluralist but not privatised, international without being subordinate to a single institutional control either in Rome or in Geneva.

We in Britain have already, on a smaller scale, faced these problems. We are endowed with a whole range of religious agencies from the Jewish Board of Deputies and Quaker meetings to the General Assembly of the Church of Scotland, General Synod and the Catholic hierarchy, all accepted as working parts of a highly pluralistic pattern of church and state. We are also endowed with a not unworkable public doctrine of twentieth century origins derived from people like Bishop Bell and Christopher Dawson and carried on still more recently by people like Barbara Ward and Gordon Dunstan. It is because of all this that the British churches should go rather confidently into Europe, determined to make our inherited resources effectively available in the larger context.

Let me give a few examples. I doubt whether anywhere else in Europe are there departments of theology so well integrated into the public university system as they are here. In Germany they are large but denominational and in some cases at least still subject to fairly un-academic ecclesiastical control; in France, in the national universities outside Strasbourg, they do not exist at all; there as in Italy, Belgium and elsewhere they are to be found only within specifically Catholic institutions, such as Leuven or the Institut Catholique. In England we have, on the other hand, a public presence of theology which has spread out from the ancient universities to many nineteenth and twentieth century foundations but is happily untied to church conditions (apart from a few chairs in Oxford and one in Durham) though not to a sense of church responsibility. Such departments are an important part of both our religious and our secular pluralism, as of a dialogue between the two. They serve the church, educating many of the clergy, purifying the ecclesiastical imagination, but also mediating religious meanings to society at large. I believe that in this and much else we have a great deal to offer Europe in a diffused and critical relationship of religion to modern society.

To take a second example, where else, in Europe today, could *Faith in the City* have been produced with its fusion of archiepiscopal commissioning, lay expertise, and pastoral follow-up? Or again consider how, just before the Gulf War began, Archbishop Runcie and Cardinal Hume went together to Downing Street to confer with the prime minister. Where else would the senior ecclesiastical leaders have either wished to speak jointly with their head of government at that moment or have been received in the natural way they were by John Major, in accordance with our whole tradition? Their visit fitted within our way of doing things, though in its precise composition it was new. That very composition signified the informal enlarging of establishment which we have already seen to be required. It also demonstrated how we have an easier ability to cross the Roman/non-Roman divide than may be discoverable elsewhere. One could offer many other examples, but these are amply sufficient to our purpose and I would question whether in France or Germany, Italy or Spain one could find any comparable range of serious ecclesiastical concern with secular issues.

A great deal of this is, undoubtedly, wholly or very considerably an Anglican and Church of Scotland inheritance. One may well judge it a spin-off of the kind of establishment which has survived, a platform for the responsible interaction of Christian thinking and secular issues, a platform in which Free Churchmen and Catholics have increasingly shared. The central symbol of this relationship of church and state is not the presence of bishops in the House of Lords but the sheer proximity of abbey to parliament, and the fruit of that proximity is not just the occasional high ritual but the informal presence maintained by Dean and Chapter. It is, of course, why people like Max Warren and Charles Gore were chosen to be canons of Westminster. It is, again, a relationship hardly to be found nowadays upon the continent but no less to be valued. That remains one focal point but it is the British relationship of church and state in all its breadth and diversity, as I have tried to portray it, which the churches in this country have now to offer to Europe. It is a tradition of critical concern for the things of this world requiring expression and development, not by some single authoritative *magisterium*, but through a constant dialogue of laity and clergy, England and Scotland, academics and bishops, Catholics and Quakers.

It is out of such mature dialogue that sane Christian contributions to our troubled world seem most likely to come, under the guidance of the Spirit and with the reflection of prayer. Such I still think was the sort of process and experience which did produce over four years the very considerable achievement of Vatican II, but which is too seldom allowed to take place within the Roman Catholic communion. There was a comparable experience in the extensive preparation for Lambeth 1988 but it was, long ago, already a characteristic of Christian life in this country and it has remained so. It was because that was the case that British Christians of two generations ago, people like J. H. Oldham and William Paton, William Temple, George Bell and Kathleen Bliss, were able to make so decisive a contribution in the early, creative, phases to the development of the Ecumenical Movement and the establishment of the World Council of Churches – a contribution well beyond that of any other nation. The European church will need that sort of British contribution tomorrow – a contribution neither nationalistic nor Ultramontane, neither authoritarian nor privatised.

If at such a moment English Christians turned instead to argue once more over the trivialities of disestablishment, they would be giving all the wrong signals and symbolically turning their back on a role which, perhaps, only they can fill. English Christians may not have seen themselves as natural Europeans. Nevertheless, George Bell may well have been the very best bishop Europe, and Germany in particular, had fifty years ago, and in the 1980s both Runcie and Hume gave a great deal of their time to Europe. In writing my biography of Runcie I was struck by the number of cities in western Europe in which he gave lectures and sermons during the course of his archiepiscopate – The Hague, Utrecht, Dublin, Brussels, Geneva, Dresden, Leipzig, Lyons, Paris, Bonn, Berlin, Lausanne, Zurich, Strasbourg as well, of course, as Rome. That list does not suggest any lack of interest in Europe, but one wonders how many British political leaders could offer anything comparable or even begin to match the manifest Europeanism of, say, Garret Fitzgerald. Fitzgerald does combine, it seems to me, the very best of what one might call Catholicism of the Maritain type, liberalism of a British sort and a complete rootedness within his own nation. That is the kind of mix we need but seldom get in this country.

One of my happiest memories is of standing beside Garret Fitzgerald in the Jesuit chapel at Miltown Park in Dublin in the early 1970s when he was Foreign Minister, and receiving communion at the hands of the Primate of the Church of Ireland but – as Garret likes to remark – even the pope has never questioned the validity of the orders of the Church of Ireland. After the same conference a German Protestant theologian came up to me, almost with tears in his eyes, to say that here for the first time in his life he had shared Communion with Roman Catholics, and how much it had meant to him. That was exceptional and it was Dublin. In England we may still not be so advanced. Fitzgerald's mother was a Protestant and he himself demonstrates the sort of fusion of Catholic and Protestant values that we have at times achieved in these islands – most notably in the life of John Henry Newman – and that we should be hoping to pass on to both the more rigidly Protestant and the more rigidly Catholic parts of Europe. We may still have, then, something of a bridge function in relation to Europe and that would be not just the role of the Church of England but of British and Irish Christianity as a whole.

Garret Fitzgerald is an Irishman and a European. We are English, Scots or Welsh, but European too. We always have been and we need to be fully in the new Europe because basically we were always part of the old Europe, even if at times since Henry VIII declared his UDI we have liked to forget it. But actually I happen to believe, being a good English patriot too, that the Europe of the 1990s is likely to need us still more, and even knows that it does so. Among other things it needs our distinctive brand of church–state relationship, the kind of politico–religious tradition I have been trying to spell out, and I very much hope that we will not let it down.

The Gore Lecture, Westminster Abbey,
13 November 1991

10

Europe and the Gospel

The faith is Europe and Europe is the faith.

Belloc's famous remark was intended in the narrowest way. 'The faith' meant Roman Catholicism and, true enough, the Europe of history is unthinkable without both Christianity and Catholicism, while the Catholicism of history is equally unthinkable without Europe. But Europe is unthinkable without a great many other things too, though it can well be claimed that Christianity, in all its diversity, has more than anything else made it what it is.

But it is precisely Christianity in its diversity which has done so, and its shaping of Europe has been done in interaction with other non-Christian influences – the pre-Christian traditions of Greece and Rome, above all, but quite other things like the continuing presence of Judaism too. Moreover, Greece and Rome shaped Christianity fairly decisively in the first place though it was then the Christian church which, again and again, ensured that Plato and Aristotle and the whole sense of Roman order, law, literature remained alive as part of an ongoing tradition, not just archaeological elements of some former, now defunct, civilisation. Christianity could do this because it has itself always been constituted as a dialogue, or, still better, a chorus of dialogues – between Hebrew scriptures and Greek scriptures, between John and Paul, between Antioch and Alexandria, between Greek churches and Latin churches. A dialogical rather than a monolithic model of Christianity is not a modern invention; it was there from the start, if temporarily outlawed by local pursuance of some rigid orthodoxy. Deepest of all has been the dialogue between Greek rationality and Hebrew faith and, hardly less pervasive, another between the Roman imperial sense and Christian otherworldliness. Christianity as an historical reality is to be seen as always both empowered and distressed by this vastly complex, almost self-contradictory, intellectual structure, a structure continually producing new antitheses and new syntheses. As such it undoubtedly shaped Europe and as the great flow of Christian experience hardened into three principal forms — Orthodox, Latin Catholic, and Protestant — so was Europe shaped like Gaul into three parts. It mattered less whether you were Celt or Teuton or Slav than whether you were Catholic or Orthodox or Protestant.

Christianity, however, was not the only religion to shape Europe, though it wished to be so and was often disgracefully intolerant of alternatives. Judaism has been an important part of Europe's spiritual heritage and so has Islam. Islam has not only just arrived, as people in Birmingham and Bradford might imagine; it has also been there in Sarajevo and Tirana and, formerly, in Cordoba for many hundreds of years. Indeed what has happened in the 1990s in Bosnia is a special tragedy for the whole of Europe because in Sarajevo, more than anywhere else in our continent, Christians and Muslims were tolerantly sharing a common society, a society in which Muslims were actually the largest group. We all needed Bosnia and, if Bosnia is destroyed, we will all be seriously the poorer.

The extraordinary diversity of Europe and of its religious character can only be properly understood if it is recognised that its three principal forms, Catholic, Orthodox and Protestant, are themselves deeply diverse. Anglicanism may be an obvious case, at least if we are viewing things from England, but the larger diversity of Protestantism from Quakers to High Church Lutherans is no less evident. The diversity of Orthodoxy may be less striking though we should not underestimate the difference between its Greek and Russian forms or, today, the contrast between Orthodoxy in its Western diaspora and Orthodoxy in its heartlands. But it is in regard to Roman Catholicism that it may be most important to stress that there always has been, and quite obviously is today, a large variety of forms. The Catholicism of the Iberian peninsula has been very different from that of the southern Netherlands, the diocese of Chur or indeed of the city of Birmingham. The Roman Catholic Ultramontane does not want to admit that — at least he only wants to admit it in terms of a culture distinct from theology or piety. In so far as he recognises it to exist, it will be in terms of defect, such as the Protestantisation of border areas, infected by uncatholic influences. But in truth such a view is unhistorical and uncatholic. Despite centuries of Ultramontane regimentation, the Catholicisms of Europe remain many and we have to be very grateful that they do: that Paris is not Rome, Louvain not the Gregorian, Benedictines not Opus Dei, and so on.

Europe is Europe because of all this, often admittedly sadly so. Much of European history is intensely miserable and much of the misery has been caused by Christian in-fighting, by the inability for instance of Christians to go on handling rationality and the Greek inheritance with requisite coolness, by sheer narrow, cruel, intolerance. That is true, but the Christianity of Europe as a cultural and historical reality, warts and all, is none the less overwhelming. Its Christianity is also, despite all the diversities, a finally unitary inheritance: you don't have to be a Catholic to appreciate Aquinas or Hopkins, a Protestant to appreciate Milton or Kierkegaard, an Orthodox to appreciate St Serafim or Dostoievski. Our Christianity is and always has been, in both its tolerances and its intolerances, at once unity and diversity and it is as such, and only as such, that Europe has historically been shaped and has become both in its extraordinary cultural richness, its profound internal divisions, its adamantine inability to cope sensibly with Belfast or the existence of the Uniates, the continent we still experience.

There has for years been a great tendency in Britain to underplay the continuing significance of religion, a tendency related to the fact that the educated class, the journalistic class especially, seems so extraordinarily ignorant of religious matters. When it discovers that, here or there, religion is important after all, it simply describes it as an expression of that overused word 'fundamentalism'. English people have, by and large, convinced themselves that religion does not matter – perhaps that was, after all, even a couple of generations ago the hidden tenet of educated politeness – at least with one proviso. In Duff Cooper's words, there were only two religions: Roman Catholicism which was wrong, and the rest which did not matter. That is why Ireland can remain so irritating, despite its charms, because there religion is still awkwardly admitted to matter whether in Belfast or in Dublin. That is why the issue of the *Satanic Verses* has been so trying and so badly handled. Here was a matter in which religion clearly did matter. In consequence the government did not know how to handle it and did not wish to know. Muslims could scream one way, liberal intellectuals the other. Despite its quite enormous significance and potential danger, it has remained a dialogue of the deaf.

In many parts of Europe religion does matter a great deal more than it matters in British suburbia. It matters because it still shapes local society. It helps make Bavaria so different from Saxony. It can matter too both explosively and destructively, but it matters primarily at the level of understanding, because as I have earlier suggested the cultural shape and development of Europe as a whole is incomprehensible without a quite close knowledge of Christian history, and of the varied forms which the Christian community has taken, the ways in which its different branches have responded both to church–state relations and to the interaction of reason and faith. Thus Orthodox Christianity never went through what we may call the medieval experience at its most formative, the rationality of the scholasticism of the thirteenth century university. Again, Catholic Christianity, at least until recently, was only marginally touched by what we may call the Reformation experience and the Enlightenment which followed it. Eastern Orthodoxy was affected still less. All these experiences were secular at least as much as religious processes and societies which never participated in them can continue to be very different from those that have.

All our traditions, however, have been profoundly dislocated by the twentieth-century continental struggle with Fascism and Communism, though it could be argued that in Britain we were much less deeply affected than in France, Germany or Holland. What came out of this struggle in the years after the Second World War was the political dominance of western Europe by what we may call Christian Democracy and of eastern Europe by Communism. At the heart of Christian Democracy as it developed in the early twentieth century, in the age for instance of Don Sturzo, and as it triumphed in the late 1940s, the age of Adenauer and de Gasperi, was the Catholic Church's current attitude to the political role of the laity for the defence and development of a Christian society. Catholicism, at least in Rome, moved pretty reluctantly to the acceptance of democracy as the natural form of government for the modern world. When it did so, it worked extremely hard and, after the collapse of Fascism, pretty successfully to ensure that the democratic process came out the way the church liked. The alternative had looked for a while like the triumph of Communism through the ballot-box – a scenario anathema alike to the pope and to the USA. It did not happen. Instead, Christian Democracy triumphed west of the Iron Curtain. East of it, the same church was basically fighting the same battle, but here the clergy were far more in the front line. Many Protestants had some sympathy for the socialist enterprise in eastern Europe; for very few Catholics was it other than diabolical. So, while Catholicism was winning the democratic battle in the West but being subtly modernised by the experience of doing so, in the East it was bearing the brunt of anti-Communist resistance and being actually hardened in the process in the most traditional attitudes.

Then came the Second Vatican Council. It would not be too far from the mark to see the enormous change wrought in Western Catholicism by the Council as the theological and liturgical equivalent to what Christian Democracy had achieved at the social and political level – the reincorporation of Catholicism, admittedly still on its own terms, in an experience pioneered by Protestants. It had been anomalous for Catholics in the 1950s, the latter years of Pius XII, to be so committed, following the example of Maritain, to Western democracy and civil freedom yet still officially denying the justification for religious freedom. To accept the latter, the process of *aggiornamento*, which had worked so effectively in democratising Catholics politically, had to become a great deal more theological than hitherto. Congar, the dissident of the 1950s, became the officially accepted prophet of renewal of the 1960s. Theology had to catch up with politics. Vatican II opened up in consequence a quite remarkable reconciliation in western Europe and elsewhere between the tradition of Catholicism and that of Protestantism. They were not reunited but they were placed in a relationship of sympathy and mutual interaction unimaginable a generation earlier.

Very little of this was experienced east of the Iron Curtain, either by Catholics or by Orthodox. There the Church of Silence, locked in battle with a decaying Stalinist imperialism, was finding its strength on the contrary in an appeal to all the most old-fashioned elements within the Roman Catholic armoury. And it won. There can be little doubt that it was Poland, the most Catholic and the most unabsorbed element in the Stalinist empire, which in the course of the 1980s proved its Achilles heel. With Karol Wojtyla as Pope and the extraordinary populist leadership and clericalist spirituality of Lech Walesa from the Gdansk shipyard, anti-Communism triumphed – in Poland, throughout eastern Europe, in the Soviet Union. To put it like that is a considerable over-simplification, though many a political analyst would not deny its large measure of truth. But what matters to us here is that this is how Catholicism views it. The church of the persecuted, the church of the martyrs, the church of Our Lady of Czestochowa has come out on top, conscious of a great mission to carry the news of its victory over Christianity's principal enemy of the twentieth century, Communism, far and wide and at the same time straighten out its feeble-willed brethren in the West who, instead of similarly overcoming the demons of liberal Protestantism and modern humanistic secularism, have largely succumbed to their softening embrace.

If Christian Europe is, as I have argued, irredeemably and wonderfully pluralist, one mighty element within that pluralism never in fact quite accepted it: the Church of Rome, in its narrowest sense, steeped in the universalist vision of Ultramontanism. It has continued to see its mission across Reformation, Counter-Reformation and the nineteenth-century revival of religion, as reunification upon its own terms: Vatican I's terms of universal dominion and a single detailed doctrinal norm. Vatican II suggested, but did not quite assert, a different model, finally leaving that of Vatican I only too clearly in place in curial minds. But where now were Rome's troops to fight for such a norm? The theologians of Louvain and Paris and Tübingen were no longer reliable. Even Bologna or Milan might come under question. Certainly in the West there were those willing still to do battle for the reunification of Christianity and Europe on a strictly monolithic and Ultramontane basis – there was Opus Dei, amongst others. Relative to the task, however, such forces, while irritating enough to fellow Catholics of more liberal persuasion, have remained negligible.

The forces of recovery might, however, providentially as it could seem, be found elsewhere. Victorious over their immediate enemy, the clergy of Poland could now pour forth, almost entirely unaffected by any of the processes which had so largely altered the face of Western Catholicism, to breathe life and hope into the campaign of recovery of traditional Roman unity and this just at the moment when Europe as a whole was at a secular level able and apparently willing to find a new unity while trying to accommodate itself to the political revolution in eastern Europe. None of this might have been very significant or have gone very far, if there had not been a Pole of vast dynamism and single-minded will occupying the See of Peter since 1978. But there has. Hence today, as Europe seeks to establish a unity which its more prosaic leaders had imagined as the unity of a fairly secular Western side of the continent, a pragmatic mix of Christian Democratic and sub-socialist presuppositions, welded together nevertheless by a fairly strong Western Catholic ideology (it was not really an accident that it all began with the Treaty of Rome and that its principal contemporary exponent Jacques Delors is a French Catholic of the firmest variety, though a member of the French Socialist Party too), much of this is being challenged not only by the recrudescence of a variety of nationalisms, but also by papal strategy. A sense of Eastern victory over twentieth-century Marxist secularism is in some way preparatory for a further victory over Western secularism and the recovery of a Christian Europe, far more religiously monolithic, far more traditionalist, far more consciously Roman, than could conceivably have been in the minds of the pragmatic bureaucrats of Brussels.

The challenge may seem unreal and in hard political terms it surely is. There are plenty of reasons for that, of which only a few need to be rehearsed here: France, eldest daughter of the church and for centuries its spiritual, missionary and theological heart, is now in reality one of the most secularised of nations, quite unable to fulfil any more its traditional Catholic role. Italy, provider of Catholicism's clerical and institutional leadership for half a millennium, is quite quickly travelling the same road. France and Italy between them have provided until the era of Vatican II the central creative tension within Catholicism, European Catholicism above all. It is gone and cannot return. In so far as Catholicism can recover its strength, it will largely be in non-European terms: African, Asian, Latin American. It is in the southern hemisphere, not Europe, that Rome's allies now lie. Even eastern Europe is far from being a series of Polands. Catholicism is far less confident and aggressive in Hungary, Lithuania or Czechoslovakia. Even in Poland, it is hard not to think that a change of religious mood is likely to come. The armies of the European Counter-Revolution of the late twentieth century may not find unlimited recruits east of the Elbe.

All this is true. Nevertheless here and now it remains clear enough, not only that a great struggle is going on within the Roman Catholic communion for the legacy of Vatican II, but also that this struggle has very considerable significance for the immediate relationship of religion to the new Europe and that the political transformation of eastern Europe has benefited the conservative side quite considerably. It is a struggle affecting all churches, as well as Europe's wider understanding of itself and of its relationship to Christianity. Pope John Paul has at times suggested that Europe breathes with two lungs, one Western and Latin, the other Eastern. It is not too clear what that other lung actually is:

Orthodox, Uniate, or just Latin Slav? Perhaps he is thinking at times of all three. And all three, it could be claimed, despite mutual hostility share a good deal in common: the absence of a major Protestant impact; the absence of a long wrestling with Enlightenment and Democracy; forty years of Communist rule, whose lasting effect was greatly to limit participation in the thought history of the rest of the world and to leave them mentally and spiritually very much where they were in the 1930s. They share a range of traditional certainties within which, for instance, the ordination of women can seem simply bizarre.

The image of two lungs is inadequate, however, to convey a sense of Europe's spiritual organism; it was and remains ever so much more complicated. The point that matters is that, while until recently we had settled into a rather static sense of Europe's shape, secular or religious, in which the complexity remained as little more than a matter of tourist interest, we have now on the contrary to adjust to a sense of ferment, of old incompatibilities crucially reawakened, of a struggle for the centre ground which might not unreasonably be compared with the long contest of the Counter-Reformation years concluded with the Treaty of West-phalia. If this is so, if we still have to work out what sort of Europe – even as regards its boundaries – we are going to be part of; what sort of religious image it is to have; then we need, first, to evaluate correctly the current form Europe's religious complexity is taking and, secondly, to assess the role that English Christianity can play within the struggle.

As to the first, it is crucial to recognise that the sharp edge of our contemporary complexity lies precisely within the Roman Catholic communion. If in any sense that matters there is a religious battle going on now which has significance for Europe as a whole, then that is the battle within Europe's principal church between, shall we say, Vatican II Conciliarists upon the one hand and Neo-Ultramontanes upon the other. On the fate of that battle almost everything else may turn in terms of Europe's Christian future. The fate of the very legacy of the Reformation today could depend less upon the churches of Protestantism than upon its creative readoption within Catholicism. If that readoption is blocked, we will all be back in the most sterile of institutional separations.

The English religious tradition has always benefited from a strikingly rich and interactive mix of Protestant and Catholic forms. You tried to extinguish Recusancy but you failed. We tried to convert you and, by and large, we failed too. But in some ways the Church of England did

133

reconvert itself to a great deal of Catholicism while John Henry Newman and a number of other remarkable converts from Anglicanism to Catholicism down to Christopher Butler did more than they realised to convert the church they had joined to the church they had left.

The Church of England needs to enter the post-1992 Europe conscious that it is both a profoundly post-Reformation church and one trying exceptionally hard to be a Catholic church on the lines of Vatican II, that its long sympathies for Rome are more important than ever, not just to itself but to everyone else, that it also has in English Roman Catholicism a sister church which it has in the past often underrated – just as it has been abused by it – but that now the two can serve Europe by sticking very much closer together than anywhere else at present do Catholic and non-Catholic churches. And this applies not just to the Church of England but to the much wider mix which has long constituted our British as well as our English Christianity. A great deal may happen in the coming years which could loosen these ties. Catholicism may be appearing to succumb more and more to the new Ultramontanism. ARCIC may become – indeed in some circles it has already become – a dirty word. It is important that such distancing should not take place and that the Church of England retains its ties both with the official Rome and with the wider, un-Ultramontane, Catholicism. A determination to keep lines open to the one should not involve playing down the significance of the other.

No less important, however, is the long-standing relationship between Anglicanism and Eastern Orthodoxy. The collapse of Communism has certainly placed its leaders in a difficult predicament, just because the long attempt to salvage something under Stalinist rule involved such a large and undoubtedly unpleasant degree of compromise, even of sycophancy. It is hardly surprising if some of the nastiest resurgences of nationalism are tied only too closely to local Orthodox churches. With their old erastian tradition, Anglicans may, perhaps, sympathise rather more with this than the rest of us can easily do. What really matters, however, is not excusing the past but building the future. It is obvious how intellectually cut off theological seminaries in Russia and throughout eastern Europe have been for generations. Perhaps the greatest service English Christianity can offer for the European churches today is to help fill in the theological and religious education of the East, not in a spirit of superiority, or with the crusading resolve to force upon them all the movements of the modernist mind, but to help with the serious undergirding of intellectual renewal, while recognising that they have a very great deal to teach us about prayer and suffering and spiritual perseverance.

The point of all this can be put simply enough: the religious state of Europe is and will remain both pluralistic and volatile. Accidents of history have shaped English Christianity not into the marginal tradition of an offshore island but into something which actually remains central to European Christianity as a whole – perhaps genuinely more central than any other of its components. It is with a real confidence in that centrality that we have to turn to Europe, not underselling the tradition we represent. To undersell it would be disastrous, not because we would be diminishing the reputation of the *Ecclesia Anglicana*, to which we all, Anglicans, Roman Catholics and Free Church people, belong, but because the Europe of many still rather rigid traditions, the Europe of Ultramontanism and Lutheranism and Calvinism and Orthodoxy, the Europe in which at present genuine ecumenism is actually receding, desperately needs doors which are kept emphatically open, points of flexibility at which Catholicism and Protestantism and Orthodoxy are seen to mingle, to the recognition of their underlying unity. I believe that nowhere else in Europe is there a national Christian tradition of which that is so true as ours. I trust it will remain true and remain useful.

A lecture given at the Birmingham Diocese Clergy Conference, Swanwick,
18 June 1992

Wiriyamu and its Aftermath

On being elected in February 1986 Portugal's first civilian president for sixty years, Mario Soares remarked in a press conference, 'The transition has ended, opening the way for a fully-fledged democracy, which is the only true source of political legitimacy.' Those words will help my reflections. It is to be remembered nevertheless that if his predecessor President Eanes was a soldier, and had indeed been Commander-in-Chief before his election in 1976 (it would really not have been possible for anyone but a military man to become President at that time), he was elected all the same in a free election and by a larger majority (61 per cent instead of 51 per cent) than that of Soares. Yet it remains true that the source of 'political legitimacy' of Eanes in 1976 was in reality at least as much military as it was democratic. It was the measure of political progress in Portugal in those ten years that the whole, rather odd, concept of a special revolutionary legitimacy enshrined in the Armed Forces Movement had quietly withered away.

The story began for me early in 1973 when, with the fairly phoney forthcoming celebration of the sixth centenary of the Anglo-Portuguese Alliance, it was arranged by the Heath Government that the Prime Minister of Portugal, Marcelo Caetano, would visit Britain in July. Those of us who were in general appalled by the current state of Mozambique, Angola and Guinea Bissau rent by a war which Portugal could never win and increasingly tied to the political and military system of South Africa, were naturally worried that the centenary celebrations would be used to bolster support for continued Portuguese rule in Africa. I was at that time a member of the Education Committee of the Catholic Institute for International Relations, whose concerns have always been largely African, and we felt we must do something significant to counter the message which was likely to come out of all this and especially out of Caetano's visit to London. We felt a particular responsibility just because the English Catholic community had long provided a pro-Salazar – as well as a pro-Franco – lobby of some effectiveness.

We decided that we would hold as public and prestigious a meeting as could be arranged, preferably in the House of Lords (Chatham House, where it actually took place, was our second choice) and as close as possible to Caetano's visit. Our plans were laid early in 1973. We decided to have three speakers. The first two choices were Lord Caradon and Mario Soares. Lord Caradon, Michael Foot's brother but rather more of an establishment figure though no less a profoundly liberal one, had been the British Ambassador to the United Nations. Soares, the leader of the Portuguese Socialist Party, was at that time in exile in Paris. His presence would make it quite clear that our protests were not anti-Portuguese but anti- the policy of Caetano's government, and his subsequent election as President thirteen years later surely finally vindicated both our conviction and our way of expressing it. We needed a third speaker, more closely identified with the CIIR itself and also more intimately concerned with Africa than was either Caradon or Soares. I was chosen to perform this role, for want of anyone better, to be a very junior member of the trio. These plans were made by March and our meeting was fixed for 11 July, as Caetano was due to arrive on the 16th. Barney Hayhoe, a Conservative MP and later Minister of Health, agreed to chair us. To be effective our protest needed an adequate cloaking of establishmentarianism.

In May of that year, visiting Rhodesia, I heard from some Spanish Burgos Fathers working there an account of the difficulties of other Burgos Fathers at work in Mozambique, in Tete province, and particularly of two priests, Alfonso Valverde and Martin Hernandez, who had by then been a year in Machava concentration camp on account of their accusations about atrocities committed by the Portuguese army near Mucumbura. I was also booked to go in June to Salamanca for an Anglican/Catholic ecumenical conference, so I arranged to call in on the Generalate of the Burgos Fathers in Madrid on the way, in hopes of obtaining more precise information which I could work into my July speech. They promised to send me copies of a number of documents. I returned from Salamanca on 22 June and received the papers early in July – a heavy bundle – but I soon picked out one highly detailed account of a quite horrifying massacre of four hundred people at and around the little village of Wiriyamu, a few miles from Tete, on 16 December 1972, as being in a class of its own. So far as I knew it was quite unpublished, it gave a reliable impression, and in the very starkness of its particularity it yet revealed only too clearly a far wider picture. I decided I should build my speech around it, and a friend translated it from Spanish to English. I received the translation on Friday 6 July and rang up Louis Heren of *The Times*, to whom I sent it next day. He rang back on the 9th to say they wished to print it at once and it appeared in full with an editorial on the 10th.

The vast storm that publication raised I cannot now properly describe. I was inevitably at its centre, responsible both for sustaining the reliability of a damning document and for interpreting the conclusions one should draw from it. It was extremely valuable, in the middle of the storm and the natural accusations that I was anti-Portuguese, to have Mario Soares beside me at the crucial meeting the day after publication. There was an immediate debate in Parliament required by Harold Wilson and within ten days I was in New York addressing a special meeting of the United Nations. Despite a barrage of denial and vituperation, Marcelo Caetano's visit was, as a result, profoundly disastrous. More and more evidence was produced in the coming months to demonstrate the extreme reliability of the report. The hard fact of Wiriyamu and the web of deceit effectually spun around it demonstrated both the inhumanity and the inefficiency of Portuguese African policy. Despite the public silence of the church at the time, it came out in due course that bishops both in Mozambique and in Portugal had indeed protested strongly about Wiriyamu well before we published our document and in fact the Patriarch of Lisbon told me later how he himself had gone with the Bishop of Quelimane to protest to Caetano.

Just nine months later the Revolution of 25 April took place. How far was Wiriyamu a contributory cause? I am of course an interested party but I continue to believe that the effect was far from insignificant. Historians have found it difficult quite to analyse why the April revolution took place when it did. All in all, from a military or an economic point of view, things were not worse then than they had been previously. In some ways, for instance militarily in Angola, they were indeed better. But the reputation of Portugal was simply in shreds. Earlier accounts of atrocities had not been confirmed to a comparable extent and, anyway, had far less of an airing. One Portuguese person later remarked to me, 'There were tears in my eyes in Lisbon on 11 July. They were not there on account of the massacre because I had known about lots of such things. They were there for the honour of my country.' Other friends in Lisbon told me how in the following months there was a growing sense of a crumbling government, failing in self-confidence. Despite the censorship a sense of what had happened slowly spread even in Portugal and may not have proved less effective than the American sense of shame over My Lai, the British over Hola. The very nature and extent of Portuguese official reactions to the report, including a delightful if sadly ill-informed work in English published by the Foreign Ministry in Lisbon and entitled *Wiriyamu, A Mare's Nest*, and the absurd cartoons depicting me even in the staid *Diario di Notitias*, were all indicative of a rather desperate sense of being cornered. But it was a cumulative matter.

I had chronicled not only army atrocities but also a growing breakdown with the church, effectively an important pillar of the colonial regime. When in April 1974 it was necessary for the government actually to deport the Bishop of Nampula from Mozambique, the degree of bankruptcy was here evident – and every such event was now exposed to major world coverage. Strangely, a long article of mine about the conflict with the church and entitled *Portugal, the Other Rebellion*, appeared in the *Observer* on 21 April, just four days before the coup and on the 23rd the *Guardian* followed that up with the publication of a confidential Portuguese officer's document confirming the facts of Wiriyamu in precise detail and naming some of the officers involved. It is, I think, obvious enough that Wiriyamu itself and the church's wider challenge linked with it had refused to go away.

The revolution of course changed everything. We, British critics of Portuguese misrule but equally friends of Portugal itself, could now sit back and watch a singularly humane, warm, imaginative transformation of the total scene. But by early 1975 it was clear that things were becoming very confused indeed. Parties were multiplying ineffectually, a dozen brands of Marxism were offering alternative solutions, while the army was digging in with hints of the development of a new military despotism closely linked with the Communist Party in the premiership of Vasco Goncalves but under the effective control of the MFA (Armed Forces Movement) and its central, if largely concealed, 'Co-ordinating Commission' (later 'Supreme Revolutionary Council'). A new censorship was being imposed. In February the CIIR asked me to go to Lisbon to try to discover what really was going on and in what way we might, perhaps, be able to help. It will certainly be hard for any historian to give an adequate account of the interminable intricacies and confusion of Portuguese politics in 1975.

I spent eight days in Lisbon between 21 February and 1 March and another four between 17 and 21 July. I seemed to spend that time in ceaseless discussion with representatives of almost every portion of the political spectrum, but, most of all, the democratic centre left. I found that everyone knew who I was, accepted me, a little oddly, as a sort of benevolent uncle of the revolution and – mostly – wanted to enlist my support for their particular brand of post-revolutionary fervour. 'Are we to have just another form of bourgeois capitalist democracy or are we to have a new society, a truly revolutionary state?' asked Teotonio Pereira of MES, one of the more extreme and delightful of Christian Marxists – he had been in prison until 26 April. Much as I liked some people of the extreme left personally, I soon concluded that theirs was not a genuine option. It was to be either military government with strong communist links and very little freedom or a liberal democratic multi-party state of a traditional western kind. Soares and the Socialist Party alone could really defend the latter and I quickly became sure that whatever support could be mustered should continue to be given to him.

The one group of people I seemed quite unable to get any interview with were the officers of the Co-ordinating Commission, try hard as I did. Then one day I was interviewed by a young journalist of *Diario Popular* and the next day (26 February) I filled its front page and there was, inside, a considerable rehash of the Wiriyamu story. It had in fact never been covered before in this way in a popular Portuguese newspaper. Almost immediately I received a request to come next day to the headquarters of the Co-ordinating Commission. Here I met two of its members, Comm. Contreiras and Barbosa Pereira. I understand that at that time Contreiras was one of the most powerful members of the MFA. They began at once by indicating their displeasure about the article on Wiriyamu. They expressed gratitude for all I had done in the past and the effect it had had, but pointed out quite frankly that far too many soldiers had been involved in atrocities. Any further publicity or enquiry would be impossibly divisive for the MFA and they had put pressure on both the United Nations and Frelimo not to inquire further into the massacres. The Armed Forces did not want to hear more about Wiriyamu. They were too compromised. Apart from that they denied that there were really any problems in the country. A young lieutenant was asked to drive me home.

The young lieutenant, however, was less discreet. We got talking and he soon insisted on taking me to dinner. As he drank more and more, I obtained a wider view of things, including the interesting information that Barbosa Pereira had told him to be very careful not to speak to me about the MFA! Indeed before the night was out he had introduced me to Senhora Arriaga, the wife of the now imprisoned General who was for long Commander-in-Chief in Mozambique and who had so over-ingenuously denied the truth of Wiriyamu.

In the subsequent months the army's grip on power became steadily more pronounced, despite the April elections in which the Socialists came easily top with over 37 per cent. In the very tense circumstances developing, I decided I must try my hand once more. Late in May (the 29th) I wrote a letter to *The Times* which was placed at the head of the page, immediately reproduced in the Portuguese service of the BBC and then reprinted in what remained of the free press in Lisbon, notably *Expresso*. A little later it was printed again in Portuguese in a collection entitled *Portugal na imprensa estrangeira – um ano depois*. I addressed the leaders of the MFA directly:

It is dangerous to exaggerate the 'legitimacy' of the Armed Forces Movement acquired by right of the revolution, just as it is specious to exaggerate the political immaturity of the Portuguese people so as to justify the long continuance of military rule. You overthrew Caetano because you alone had the guns. You deceive yourselves if you think this gives you an enduring guarantee to be the true spokesmen for the mass of the nation ... The Portuguese people have given no evidence of wanting semi-permanent military rule nor a third-world style single political party, the civil branch of the military, and if you commit yourselves to such a line you will, little by little, find yourselves as unpopular and as necessarily tyrannical as Salazar and his unique party, the *Uniao Nacional*. Despite your good intentions and genuine reforms, you would then have proved yourselves the heirs and not the destroyers of fascism.

Do not forget your own past record. While Mario Soares and Alvaro Cunhal were in prison or exile, you were carrying out the African policies of Salazar and Caetano. As you know only too well, the greatest atrocities of their regime were in Africa, and the army was deeply involved – so deeply that since April 1974, you have never been able to investigate them yourselves. Many of you know why. Do not imagine that the spirit of fascism has been wholly eradicated from your own spirit by some flick of a left-wing wand.

Soares later told me on two separate occasions how important he thought that letter had been. It was, perhaps, because of it that I was invited to attend in July an international conference on *Socialism and Freedom* mounted to provide support for Soares in an ever-more critical situation. I was in fact the only person from Britain who responded to the invitation and I found myself for a few days part – if clearly a rather idiosyncratic part – of an inner group of international socialists including Gilles Martinet, André Boulloche and Michel Achilli. In a special discussion between us which was reproduced in full in two issues of *Jornal Novo*, I remarked that it seemed to me that while the political leaders were more concerned to have a socialist Portugal than a democratic Portugal, the greater part of the population was far more anxious to have a democratic Portugal than a socialist Portugal.

On the night of Saturday 19 July we all attended a truly vast demonstration in the centre of Lisbon in which Soares called for the dismissal of Vasco Goncalves. Large as it was, it seems that many people from the country were prevented by army road blocks from attending. A group of foreign members of the conference were with Soares on the platform. We were introduced and embraced by him one by one and, while most of the government-controlled press paid very limited attention to the demonstration, reaffirming instead the support of the *povo* for Goncalves, *A Capital* did publish a provocative photograph of Mario and myself both embracing and greeting the crowd. Perhaps it was meant to indicate how the Socialist Party was in reality hand-in-glove with the church.

If the Communist Party regarded that as condemnation, for the Socialist Party it was in truth an important part of its strategy. The next day, Sunday, the conference listened to nearly an hour's speech from the old Bishop of Oporto. Of all the oddities of that strange time, this must have been one of the most striking. He had a unique position of respect in the country – the one liberal voice in the church, a man who had for years been exiled by Salazar. But his was indeed an old-fashioned liberalism with a very real social conscience but absolutely no trace of socialism about it. The Socialist Party, however, needed all the support it could muster and they listened most deferentially as he rambled on and on about St Paul and Rousseau. The foreign socialists – French, German and

Italian – looked extremely bored and protested later that it was odd for socialists in a socialist state to be expected to listen to an hour's sermon from a bishop. The Portuguese, on the contrary, were immensely pleased to have him. It demonstrated the compatibility of socialism and the church. They were in fact on a tight-rope, needing on the one hand not to renege on their socialist and revolutionary legitimacy within what were then the dominant left-wing circles of power and ideological rhetoric, while at the same time they had to establish their genuinely democratic and indeed liberal legitimacy if they were to obtain the mass support of a far more conservative population which was the principal card they could play against the military.

In fact they succeeded and I am glad they did. The government of Portugal may not have been particularly stable in the next ten years but I am sure it would have been a good deal worse if the early military ideologues of the post-revolutionary period had had their way. In fact they crumbled after the mismanaged coup of Carvalho of November 1975. Eanes became President, Soares Prime Minister and the course was slowly set for the entry of a democratic Portugal into the European Community. The revolution and military power could not provide the sort of legitimacy the country both needed and craved – and without which it could but remain isolated in Europe both culturally and politically. There has been a plethora of elections since and most Portuguese people may be sick and tired of them, but they have firmly established the basic fact of democratic legitimacy in traditional Western terms, and the election of Soares as President was a suitable conclusion to the whole process at the moment when entry to the EEC had at last been obtained, for he more than anyone else stood committed to this all along, just as he was no less committed to the ending of the Portuguese African Empire.

After 1975 I moved deliberately away from further involvement in this lengthy process, but I am happy to recall the small part I played for a while in the pursuit of democratic legitimacy, and to be able to conclude that if in July 1973 I was branded as an enemy of Portugal, I in fact, as I always claimed, was very much a friend, and one both supported by, and able to support, the man who was eventually to become its first civilian president since the 1920s.

It may seem very odd that an English priest was able to enter the Portuguese political process in the 1970s in any way at all. If in fact I did so rather successfully it was, of course, initially because of Portugal's African dimension and my access to sources of African information from which the Portuguese themselves had been systematically excluded. It was, I would judge, a combination of accurate information, sound political analysis and sheer passion which made it possible to be prophetic, and yet prophetic in an essentially liberal and moderate cause. Once the situation changed, my job, such as it was, inevitably and totally came to an end.

Opposing Salazar and Caetano did not mean being an enemy of Portugal, just as opposing Nazism in the 1940s did not mean being an enemy of Germany. On the contrary, for my own part I well remember my impassioned defence of the existence of 'Good Germans' at that time against those who denied there could be any such thing. Today in the 1990s when one raises one's voice in defence of the people of Bosnia, one is accused of being anti-Serbian. It is again untrue. There were indeed British nationals in the 1940s, inspired by Lord Vansittart, for whom Germans as such were the enemy. For many Croats, alas, the Serbs as such are the enemy today. Governments can be a true enemy if their policies are ones of aggression, racialism and injustice, but not whole peoples. Those who struggled against the governments of Germany fifty years ago, Portugal twenty-five years ago and Serbia today are not – if they are true to the cause – enemies but friends of Germany, Portugal and Serbia. They are friends of Hans von Dohnanyi and Dietrich Bonhoeffer, of Mario Soares, of Miro Lasavic, the Serb President of the Bosnian Parliament. Justice and an emotional response, for or against, to a specific people, have very little to do with one another.

Lecture given at the Portuguese Week, University of Leeds, 21 February 1986, revised September 1994

12

Bosnia and the Churches

I have never been to Bosnia or to any other part of former Yugoslavia and I have had no personal interest in it whatever. Yet I have come since 1991 to give a great deal of time and energy to crying out to an indifferent world the truth about Bosnia as I see it, a truth not just about mass murder, rape and the attempted genocide of an entire society but about the sustained collusion of the British Government and the United Nations Secretariat in what is going on: the greatest public crime in post-Second World War European history. If numerous other, better informed and more influential people had been saying the same, I would have felt no special obligation to do so. It is because they have not been, because there has been a glaring absence of outcry on the part of the academic, artistic, literary, ecclesiastical and political establishment that I have found it incumbent upon me to do what I could. I have in consequence written as many letters and articles in the press as I could muster, I have spoken in Trafalgar Square and at public meetings in Liverpool, Manchester, Birmingham, Bradford, Leeds and elsewhere, I have produced three editions of a booklet *SOS Bosnia*, and I have appeared as often as invited on radio and television.

I have been greatly heartened as I learnt more about Bosnia and developed my own analysis to find it almost entirely in accord with that of a number of people who knew far more about it than I did. I am referring to Branca Magas, author of *The Destruction of Yugoslavia*, Mark Thompson, author of *A Paper House: The Ending of Yugoslavia*, Noel Malcolm, author of *Bosnia: A Short History*, Mark Almond, author of *Europe's Backyard War*, Bogdan Denitch, author of *Ethnic Nationalism: the Tragic Death of Yugoslavia*, Professor John Fine, author with Robert Donia of *Bosnia and Herzegovina: A Tradition Betrayed*, and Marshall Harris, until his resignation responsible in the State Department in Washington for the Bosnia desk. There is simply no comparable alternative analysis. The ignorance, avoidance of central issues of history and justice, the pomposity and smugly patronising pretence to be trying to do one's best with impossible Balkan types which characterise, for instance, the speeches of Douglas Hurd and David Owen have, on the contrary, simply reinforced my conviction that something very nasty is going on, not only in Bosnia but throughout the corridors of Western power.

The Bishop of Worcester, replying to my 1994 article in *Theology* (see below), has written that I cannot be so naive as to think that there is only one view a Christian can take in regard to Bosnia. As regards essentials, I willingly confess to being so naive as to believe just that. The fate of the Jews at the hands of Hitler presented no less and no more clear an issue in the 1930s: what then, as now, could truly be judged a *status confessions*, an issue so basic that the church is required of its very nature to commit itself at the pain of ceasing to be truly the church. The incontestable essentials include, I suggest, the following:

1   The war in Bosnia, following on that in Slovenia and Croatia as well as the originating Serb subjugation of Kosova, is entirely the product of Serb nationalism and aggression.
2   The war has been waged against a people, its culture and religion; in intention and in many places in execution it has been truly genocidal, genuinely comparable with the Holocaust.
3   There have been no remotely comparable crimes committed upon the Bosnian side.
4   The Serb Orthodox Church and its bishops have overwhelmingly backed the campaign of aggression.
5   The attack upon Bosnia is a blatant violation of the United Nations Charter, to which the Bosnian Government has again and again appealed.
6   The Arms Embargo, imposed upon the Bosnian government and people by the United Nations and defended above all by the British Government, has severely affected their ability to exercise their right of self-defence and is inherently immoral and illegal.
7   Strong military action, especially from the air, undertaken by NATO or the UN, could quickly have ended the war in 1992 or at any time since.

8   All the settlements proposed by the West – the Owen-Vance plan, the Owen-Stoltenberg Plan, and the Contact Group Plan – are profoundly unjust, unnecessary and unhelpful for a stable future. All derive equally from sustained Western, and especially British, determination to see Bosnia divided in favour of the Serbs.

9   That no effective international action has ever been taken, except to stop the shelling of Sarajevo after the Market Place massacre in February 1994, is above all the responsibility of the British Government, determined that Serbia should not be forced to withdraw from the greater part of its gains.

Seldom has such evil been done and done so publicly. If proof be needed of the anaemia from which the British churches suffer at present it can be found in the failure to conduct a clear analysis or to raise their voices against this huge crime and the collusion with it of our own government. The following three pieces were published, one for each year of the war, as an appeal to the churches to think again; an appeal which, sadly, has gone almost unheeded.

The *Tablet*, August 1992

The greatest human disaster to have happened in Europe since the Second World War is taking place in Bosnia; the most ruthless and calculated aggression not just against a state but against a people: large-scale massacre, the herding of tens of thousands of ordinary people into concentration camps, sealed trains and exile. Why? Because they are not Serbs. This recrudescence of racist nationalism of the crudest type is a mirror image of the Nazi treatment of the Jews. Only this time the victims are Muslims.

Bosnia is an independent country recognised by both the European Community and the United Nations. Its government has followed a policy backed by the large majority of its citizens and in no way discriminatory against the rest. It has appealed repeatedly for help from the world community against aggression and genocide. The people of Bosnia have lived together for centuries in a completely mixed way and no policy of 'cantonisation' (which in effect is a mere subterfuge for handing over large parts of the country to Serbia) could possibly do justice to such a community. Moreover its imposition would be a betrayal of a European ideal of pluralism, an ideal which it is ironically the Muslims who are defending. What has destabilised Bosnia has been the rise of a Serb racialist nationalism espoused by Milosevic and the plan to create a 'greater Serbia' by 'ethnic cleansing' of large areas which never have been Serbia. The government of Bosnia is not then standing for the rights of Muslims alone. It is standing for Bosnia's historic character as an open society in which Muslims and Christians live freely together. Nowhere else have Muslims been more open, more friendly, more integrated into the European world.

The vicious attack by a nominally Christian group upon a Muslim community will enormously increase the pressure towards fundamentalism in Islam all across the world and will immensely damage Europe's own resources for reconciling Muslim and non-Muslim. It is a religious as well as a human tragedy of the first order.

Britain has, sad to say, the greatest responsibility for the failure to respond to Bosnia's pleas for help. The British Government has consistently impeded the giving of effective assistance through insisting on a continuation of Lord Carrington's wholly ineffectual role and arguing mistakenly that this is a war internal to Bosnia. Essentially it is not. The Serbian minority within Bosnia is seizing control simply through the services of the planes, heavy artillery and tanks of the former Yugoslav army controlled and manned from Belgrade.

What have the churches done to speak out in defence of Bosnia, of its peace-loving Muslim community and against a revival of the most virulent racism? There appears to have been a most striking silence from all the principal church leaders in Britain. It will go down in history. We pour out our tears at the Holocaust but close our eyes to the Holocaust happening in 1992. 'Only he who shouts for the Jews may sing the Gregorian chant', declared Bonhoeffer fifty years ago. Only he who shouts for the Bosnian Muslims is entitled to do so today.

The *Guardian*, July 1993

Bosnia has exposed the moral and ideological bankruptcy of Western society more devastatingly than anything this century, even Nazism. The evils are comparable. Yet, while we know far more about what is going on, we have done far less.

Splendid as have been the efforts of the smaller relief agencies, the political response – and especially the presence of Unprofor – has been a well-devised cover-up for inactivity. The genocide of a European people has continued for over a year, and Europe has done nothing to stop it when it could have ended it – and still could end it – within a week. For this our political leaders (and most especially the government of Britain, which has orchestrated the world's reaction from first to last) will for ever bear the shame.

This has been possible only because almost every other side of society has failed to express any real sense of outrage. This is true of the Labour Party, of the academic community and even of the media.

The silence of church leaders in this country has been, if anything, even more striking. Yet it is precisely when the normal mechanisms of society are failing to guard the values of humanity that the church is needed. That remains its supreme social justification: to be a prophetic voice, the voice of the voiceless, the unsilenceable defender of the poor and of justice. If those in need are mostly Muslims who have lived peaceably for generations with their Christian neighbours but are now being destroyed by nominal Christians, that is all the more reason for Christians to come to the rescue. Yet what has the Archbishop of Canterbury or of York had to say, or the Cardinal Archbishop of Westminster, or the Council of Churches of Britain and Ireland? What a silence have we been treated to at this the greatest outrage of post-war European history! Bishop George Bell of Chichester was a lonely voice fifty years ago when he spoke up for the Jews. Where is a Bishop of Chichester today?

Why are Christian leaders behaving like this? The first reason is the perennial parochialism whereby most church people remain preoccupied with the parish pump (and, when tens of thousands of Bosnian women are being systematically raped, the ordination of women is a parish pump issue). The second reason is a misguided ecumenism. Anglicans in particular are anxious to remain on good terms with the Orthodox, and the Serbian Orthodox Church has had closer relations with the Church of England than any other. It is also doing a very great deal to fuel Serb nationalism. To take a strong line against Serb aggression could be to displease one's Orthodox friends. Better to stress instead that this is a complex matter and there must be wrongs on every side.

Thirdly, a misguided pacifism which can eat the guts out of an effective Christian political stance. Few Christians are really pacifist. Most of the clergy who were in the Peace Pledge Union in 1938 were in uniform by 1940. But many like to think that pacifism is best so long as their own homes are not threatened. To justify their position they almost always play down the reality of evil, misread reality, claim that a Goebbels or a Karadzic is not really as bad as all that. If someone is a complete pacifist and would be prepared to see their own children butchered by a terrorist rather than intervene, then so be it. But there are few such people.

And even they have no right to deny arms to other people desperately endeavouring to defend their families and homes. For the rest of us who are not pacifists and never have been, to refuse either to intervene and use our military might to save a small nation which has appealed to us for help or allow them arms to help themselves against the equivalent of something far worse than the IRA, is morally wicked, thoroughly soft thinking and wholly unChristian. If the church had spoken out, not once but daily, if our archbishops had insisted on going to Sarajevo and staying there, sharing the life of its bombarded people, then our government would never have persevered in its course of studied determination to prevent any effective resistance to aggression.

The church is not so weak, if it would only venture its strength. It might actually have stopped the war, achieved the fruits of a true pacifism – a concern for peace which could actually bring peace.

The claim, regularly heard, that there is nothing we can do which is likely to end the war, is baseless. The Serb attack on Croatia stopped once force was met by adequate force. Again, the moment it looked as if Milosevic would genuinely pressurise Karadzic to end the war was the moment when there was a serious threat of American military action. At that point the war was close to ending. However, British pressure quickly removed the American threat.

When force is met with force, the war will end. It is Britain and the UN which are ensuring it continues by refusing either to stop it or to allow Bosnians their natural right – the arms to defend themselves.

Sadly, it has from the start been British policy that a Greater Serbia should be created and Bosnia destroyed. And church leadership in this country, by its erastian inability to challenge that policy, has colluded, and is colluding in the crime.

Theology, July 1994

Reflecting on the response of the churches in Britain and within the Ecumenical Movement to Bosnia once more, I remain appalled by how little they have done at the level of their leadership to recognise without ambiguity what has been happening, to condemn what is evil and above all to offer any significant support to a European nation oppressed in a way unprecedented since 1945.

Again and again church leaders in this country have been urged to visit Sarajevo, to show some really significant degree of human and religious solidarity with the Muslim community of Bosnia in its ordeal. They have entirely failed to do so. Almost the only church leader to have spoken emphatically enough to be heard has been the Bishop of Barking, to whom all praise for his willingness to stand up and be counted, even in Trafalgar Square. For the rest one has received the sort of avoidance reply typified by a spokesman of Lambeth Palace in response to the suggestion that Archbishop Carey, having visited the Sudan, could now highly appropriately go to Bosnia: 'There are no Anglicans in Sarajevo.'

Three documents illustrate what the churches have said. The first is a 27-page report of the Council of Churches of Britain and Ireland on Serbia and Croatia, January–February 1993; the second a message adopted by the Central Committee of the World Council of Churches at its meeting in Johannesburg, 20–28 January 1994; the third a speech by the Bishop of Worcester in the House of Lords debate on Bosnia, 14 February 1994.

Take the CCBI report first. From its opening line it purports to be about 'former Yugoslavia'. Its delegation took place at a time when war between Croatia and Serbia was over but the attack on Bosnia at its worst, yet it decided to 'confine itself to Serbia and Croatia'. It visited Belgrade and Zagreb (for no more than a week in all) but nowhere in Bosnia. It has many interesting and thoughtful things to say but it avoids any serious political analysis as to why this war has broken out or what, in objective terms, might be just or unjust. While its Bosnian and Muslim contacts are marginal, it still manages to insert into its 'Conclusion and Recommendations', without the slightest serious examination of the pros and cons, the suggestion that military intervention in Bosnia is unlikely to be justified. The delegation was briefed in advance by the Foreign Office and stayed in Belgrade at the British Residence. When it had so little time in all to hear a divergence of views from anyone else, and spent less than forty-eight hours even in Zagreb, it was hardly a balanced way to come to an understanding of the situation. Certainly the view the delegation expressed was the view the Foreign Office wished to hear. Apart from that, the central fact remains that at the time a crusade of extermination, human and cultural, was being carried on by Serbs against Muslims, a

British church delegation took as its priority to visit Serbia and Croatia and concentrate upon the ecclesiastical tension between the two. This seems to me a glaring example of what churches ought not to do in a time of political crisis.

The second example is very much worse. Seldom has the World Council performed more discreditably than in its Johannesburg message. It first declares that 'much of the reporting of the conflict lacks objectivity' (the reporting has, on the contrary, for the most part been outstandingly objective, the one redeeming element in the West's response to the crisis) and adds that 'violence and brutality are being committed on every side, Serb, Croat and Muslim' (all the evidence is that there has been systematic genocide and rape on the Serb side from the start; that what has been done by Muslims has been in retaliation, unplanned and on a vastly much smaller scale). There is no further reference to Muslims whatsoever. It then goes on to speak of the 'desperate shortage of food and medical supplies' in Serbia and Montenegro which has 'caused widespread suffering to the civilian populations' without the slightest reference to the fact that the shortage of food, medical supplies and every necessity of life – let alone the constant bombardment from Serb artillery – is infinitely worse in Bosnia. It manages never once to make use of the word 'Bosnia'. Unsurprisingly, the message goes on to oppose armed intervention, in this as in everything else reflecting a militant Serb viewpoint, toned down with suitable talk of the need for reconciliation. Seldom has a message of the World Council so entirely abandoned a theology of liberation and of justice.

Thirdly, the speech of the Bishop of Worcester. It was the only speech by a bishop in the House of Lords debate and it is to be presumed that it had been cleared at Lambeth. It reflected only too clearly every piece of mistaken analysis used to justify doing nothing to save Bosnia from aggression over almost two years. First, the bishop was careful to stress that this was a civil war when in reality it is primarily a war of aggression. Then, almost laughably, he repeated the well-worn assertion that it would take 130,000 men, if not more, to save the city of Sarajevo from the guns of the soldiers surrounding it. He went on to add that he did not believe it right nor wise to make air strikes. I say 'laughably' because that very week General Rose and a NATO threat of air strikes had made Sarajevo safe from shelling, without any additional men and without the loss of a single life, for the first time in eighteen months. Logically it must be presumed that the bishop would have preferred the massacre in the market place to have continued on a daily basis. In fact, of course, he simply had not thought out what he said. His speech was just one more example of poor analysis, acceptance of a Foreign Office viewpoint by church leaders and – underlying that – of Serb claims. It is remarkable that the Bishop of Worcester referred at length to all the good things he claimed the churches were doing in the war, beginning with the Orthodox, but never at any point made mention of Muslims. Is this really why we have bishops in the House of Lords?

The overall impression of these and other documents is of an amazing inability to face up to the reality of evil and to grapple responsibly and clear-mindedly with a moral crisis comparable to the Holocaust. On the one hand the ecumenical desire not to upset the Serb Orthodox Church and, on the other, willingness to swallow whole the political line of the Foreign Office and the European Community, have completely nullified any prophetic voice on the part of central church leadership. Sadly it reveals how low the organised Ecumenical Movement has sunk. This year there is a special celebration for Bishop Bell in Chichester Cathedral. Was there ever a more glaring example of building monuments to the prophets when they are well dead? A Bishop Bell in 1994 would have been quite a different matter.

13

Judaism in Today's World

One of the great heroes of my life has been Robert Grosseteste, the thirteenth-century scientist and theologian, Chancellor of Oxford University and from 1235 until his death in 1253 the Bishop of Lincoln. He was, unquestionably, one of the most remarkable of medieval figures. A man of the poorest origins who went to the very top of society; a scientist who turned to theology in middle life and then to a theological methodology including the study of Greek which was quite uncharacteristic of mid-thirteenth-century theologians; a highly pastoral bishop who was only ordained a priest in his fifties and who died in his eighties, denouncing papal misrule with strange prophetic fervour.

There is much to think about in Grosseteste, much to admire, much to be somewhat bewildered by, but I have to confess that I only really came to understand him at all adequately when in 1986 Sir Richard Southern published his superb study of 'the Growth of an English Mind in Medieval Europe', to use the subtitle of his biography. It has, however, made my tendency to hero-worship Grosseteste a great deal more difficult because of his quite exceptional degree of hostility to the Jews of his time. Jews were not well treated in thirteenth-century England but by most people they were tolerated, by some protected – for good motives and bad. There were friendships, conversations, even conversions of Christians to Judaism as of Jews to Christianity. If there were fierce eddies of popular hostility, many churchmen did their best to mitigate them, including an earlier bishop of Lincoln, St Hugh. Not so Grosseteste. As Archdeacon of Leicester he seems to have been responsible for persuading its earl, a friend of his, the young Simon de Montfort, to expel the Jews from the town in 1232. But he did not stop there. The Countess of Winchester had welcomed the exiles to her town, and this act greatly annoyed Grosseteste who wrote her a letter of fierce reproof and condemnation for her hospitality. The uncompromising rigidity and verbal violence with which he spelt out the anti-Jewish attitudes of contemporary Christianity may have been personal to himself but they did, doubtless, add their mite to the general growth of anti-semitism which led to the expulsion of all Jews from England sixty years later.

I refer to this not because it is anything very unusual in the history of Christianity or of Europe, but because of its personal significance for me. Probably none of us, when admiring some aspect of the work or personality of a figure of the past, is aware of all other significant sides of his or her persona or would not be distressed by some part of them upon discovery. Our retention of the past and ability to identify with aspects of it is inevitably highly selective and even fictitious. Grosseteste was both an outstandingly independent thinker and singularly uncompromising in pursuit of any line which he had really taken up. One can see this trait in his quarrels with the chapter of Lincoln and the pope himself; his harshness towards the Jews is very much of a piece with the rest of him. Yet my tardy discovery of this harshness has forced me to meditate anew upon the corroded quality of the tradition of which I have seen myself as part, including aspects of the culture of modern English Catholicism.

If my childhood home in Oxford was quite exceptionally open to many Jewish refugees from Germany and Czechoslovakia – just as it was to German prisoners-of-war – a reflection of both the Christianity and liberalism of my parents, I also imbibed unthinkingly chunks of anti-semitism from what one might call Chester-Belloc culture which only slowly did I recognise for what they were, and reject. We can recognise today more easily and far less controversially than a generation ago how profoundly European Christian culture has been affected by anti-semitism. For every one of us, from every tradition and background, when we come to face with honesty the religious and cultural tradition to which we belong, in its almost unendurably smug totality, it is bound to be a very painful business. Yet there can be no escape from it, if we are to enter with spiritual and intellectual integrity into living with, serving, understanding and even speaking the truth in love, to people of very different backgrounds and commitments.

All this has set me thinking anew about the inherent condition of diaspora Jewry, the state of being a politically defenceless minority. It has been throughout most of history the normative condition of Judaism and it has not always, or necessarily, been an unhappy condition. I would like to examine that condition theologically and historically but, first, I will recall one other example of a Christian–Jewish encounter, an incident in Ethiopia in the sixteenth century concerning a Falasha and a Stephanite monk. The Falasha were a group of Ethiopians who had over the years, in a way that is hidden from us, come to a substantially Jewish faith and were, at times at least, described as Jews. The incident in question is described in the life of the monk, Abba Gabra Masih, and it was composed shortly after his death. The Stephanite monks were frequently persecuted for deviating from various details of Ethiopian orthodoxy and Gabra Masih was, at the time, alone in refuge, in a state of great exhaustion. The Falasha, finding him in this condition, carried him on his back to his house and 'fed him like a baby', caring for him for five months until Gabra Masih had fully recovered. Then the monk, to quote from his *gadl* or biography,

> cried in front of that Jew remembering his father and his brothers whose fate he did not know because he had left them in a great persecution ... And he (the Falasha) said to him 'Stay with me in your manner. I will give you food, water, clothes and vegetables. All which your heart desires I will do for you, either in secret or openly.' And he (Gabra Masih) said to him, 'May God bless you but bid me farewell ... I wish to join with my brothers in crucifixion and death and everything which happens to them.'[1]

This lovely story of the befriending by a Jew of a Christian monk persecuted in a Christian country explicitly refers to the teaching of Moses 'Love your neighbour as yourself' (Leviticus 19:8) as the ground for the Falasha's behaviour, thus demonstrating a sense of a shared religious tradition as well as a shared humanity, the conscious possession of common scriptures. Grosseteste was actually commenting upon the Psalms at the time of the Jewish expulsion from Leicester. If he paused to consider that these people prayed exactly the same Psalms which meant so much to him, it would, I fear, only have increased his bitterness towards them. Just as civil war can be the most bitter of wars so schism can be the most bitter of religious divisions, but it is still division within a family and it is pleasant to see in our Ethiopian story how that sense of shared revelation and moral norm was alive between two black men in a society far less developed academically than thirteenth-century England.

The story also suggests how the common condition of being a minority, unprivileged by the state, made sympathy easier. Grosseteste lived in a very self-consciously Christian society in which church and state were closely integrated. The city of God was identified as the church here present. The Jews were the one apparently unintegrated element of humankind. The fundamental inability to be integrated into the Christian model of western European society as it had developed in the post-Constantinian age under the leadership of popes, emperors and theologians alike, forced them into increasing isolation, most of all when the inherent logic of the age was applied so unyieldingly as it was by Grosseteste.

It was really when Christendom itself began to fall apart at the Reformation that pressure on the Jews was lessened. The Reformers themselves did not necessarily see it like that. No one was more fiercely anti-Jewish than Martin Luther. Yet the consequence of their movement was by and large to decrease the monism of religion and society which had submerged the dualism of early Christianity. There would be increasing room for diversity even though the Reformation's immediate consequence was actually in places to enhance the monist ideal, simply substituting a national church for the international church. But in the longer term, in a Europe of many nations large and small, this could only lead to acceptance of pluralism, of a multiplicity of churches and beliefs. Jews re-entered the scene and could belong to it almost as naturally as Quakers or Unitarians. The British state at least found it no harder to accept Jews to citizenship than Roman Catholics.

A conviction of the unity of church and state died hard – many a Spanish Catholic, Serb bishop and unreconstructed Anglican still pines for what was a deeply damaging importation into the fourth century church. The close linking of belief with the political power of a state was characteristic of the ancient world but it was deeply antipathetic to the natural dualism of early Christianity – something inherited at least in part from the diaspora condition of first-century Jews – and the Constantinian establishment of Christianity damaged the latter in all sorts of ways, not least in encouraging and institutionalising all the more negative sides of its relationship with Judaism. And what had been a quite loose linking of religion and empire in the Greece or Rome of antiquity became with Christianity quite quickly a rather tight one. Only in the condition of modern pluralism have Christians been freed from the Constantinian legacy to see how it impaired their spiritual inheritance, in no way more than in their approach to other religious traditions. A confident sense, even one held unsaid, of possessing political supremacy, is unlikely to be of assistance in religious dialogue.

Those reflections lead to my central theme – the relationship of Judaism and the state. It may not be pointless for Jews to be reminded of the Christian church's long problem of retaining its moral freedom *vis à vis* a state committed to its public support. For two millennia Jews had no such political institution to identify with or to provide them with even minimal protection. Their insecure and perennially intimidated existence, quite apart from and previous to the Nazi Holocaust, led naturally and logically to the nineteenth-century dream of re-establishing a homeland and protective political institutions. The mass return to Palestine and re-creation of Israel embraced both a political and a religious logic. Circumstances in due course also favoured it and the statelessness of the Jews which had underlain their predicament for so many centuries has been decisively overcome. Thus were some problems solved but others inevitably created as is the way of all history. The consequent political problems of the Middle East will not be our concern here but the religious implications of some of them will be.

Of its very nature the re-establishment of Israel forces Jews to consider, as they had rather little need to do until recent decades, the proper relationship between the religious and the political community; to consider, that is to say, an issue with which Christians have had to wrestle for a very long while, and often ruefully. It was of course easy enough and understandable enough to find in the Hebrew Bible an account of a single community, religious and political, with its capital in Jerusalem and to wish to re-establish it in its fullness, but it is wholly impossible to model a twentieth-century institution upon a tenth-century BC institution. Both the national and religious community have moved on immeasurably, and it is clear, to take one very obvious example, how little desire there is to rebuild the temple, which would then entail reconstituting the ritual life of the temple, and even substituting priests for rabbis in the religious leadership. Again, politically, if Israel exists fairly safely today, it does so because of its alliance with the United States, and if we were to fit the United States into a model of two and a half millennia ago, it would certainly have to be as Babylon, or later, as Rome – hardly a very satisfactory role from a Jewish viewpoint.

It is, however, ridiculous even to try to make such equivalences. The Jewish community, like the world community, has moved immeasurably onward. Judaism, as the living religion of today, the Judaism of Mishnah and Talmud but also of living twentieth-century people sharing in the humanistic and scientific culture of the ongoing world to a very great and quite inevitable extent, never was until the second half of the twentieth century the religion of an independent political community; it was the religion of a dispersed monotheist nation. It seems to me that the dispersion was more than an accident and much more than a disaster. It was a consequence of the very strength of Judaism as a religion but it was also a condition for its continued survival, a morally significant and exclusive monotheism in a non-Christian and non-Muslim form. No kingdom of the ancient world has survived. Judaism did so because of its ability to escape political and geographical limitation while remaining true to its essential self.

The dispersion was not simply, or perhaps primarily, the consequence of Babylonian, Greek or Roman conquest. The mobility of people of every race has been far greater than most of us realise, but migrants are rather easily absorbed into their communities of adoption, so that they seldom survive long as a recognisably independent human group unless they are held back from such identification by the power of religion or, occasionally, of race, though the latter is far more questionable. Without any doubt over the centuries large numbers of Jews have been wholly absorbed into every European nation and certainly their race did not impede it, but if as a group they have not been absorbed it is for a religious reason: the sheer power, spiritual and intellectual, of the Hebrew scriptures and the post-biblical synagogical and ritual functioning of Judaism. In this way Judaism became and has remained a genuinely world religion. But you cannot be a world religion and a state religion at the same time and in the same way. Nothing can excel the Hebrew scriptures in their sheer theological insight, their poetic and moral power, their literary range. Very little of that remains tied to the political experience of a small, poorly governed, middle eastern state which lasted a few hundred years. To say that is not to deny the providential significance of that state which was indeed a catalyst for much of the greatest biblical literature. But the Bible survived at the core of a living community of belief through the fidelity and courage of countless human beings unprotected by the power of a state.

Lack of protection had some extremely dire consequences, but it also had more positive religious ones than we may recognise. And, as a human condition, it was not of course unique. Many racial and cultural groups have had to survive and still have to without the support of a state of their own – though very seldom without the support of land. It was in being almost landless, rather than in being stateless, that the Jewish experience was (apart from that of the Gypsies) very nearly unique. What made it nevertheless possible was the transcendence and universalism of a great religion. Jews may be fortunate today to have again both land and a state, though for many of us the latter is a more dubious blessing. The pursuit of the nation state has been one of Europe's more disastrous cul-de-sacs. It has not served the world well and, while it is easy enough to see why the Croats, for instance, or the Slovenes, want one, we have, I believe as a world community, for the sake of a peace which can embrace and be secure for everyone, to renounce the false security of the nation state. I suspect that in due course this will prove to be true also for Israel, but it is in terms of the survival of Judaism as a living world religion and not in terms of political wisdom that I want here to suggest caution in regard to the likely consequences of the nation state.

The logic of Israel's modern history has, increasingly, been the logic of the Return, a logic which must inevitably in some way undermine the existence of Jews everywhere else. Moreover, the extremely confrontational character of that history and the widely perceived sense of a need for solidarity on the part of all Jews with Israeli government policies – a solidarity of course by no means fully achieved either inside or outside Israel – have made a relationship of critical distance between religion and state policy particularly difficult to maintain. Yet it was precisely the value of such a distance which the prophetic tradition at its height most powerfully demonstrated.

There are two issues here: the relationship between Judaism as a religion and the modern State of Israel, and the relationship of the diaspora Jewish community to the State of Israel.

I speak to these two issues as a concerned outsider, though a Christian can hardly be a complete outsider. Much of the Christian Bible is identical with the Jewish Bible. The Psalms have remained the heart of Christian devotion and for many years I recited the entire Psalter weekly. There were times when Christian monks endeavoured to recite it daily; now they do so monthly! Fervour may decline but the principle is unchanged. It is a witness to the spiritual bond still uniting across two thousand years the two sides of a religious schism which developed among Jews in the wake of the life and death of Jesus of Nazareth. Every time the Western Catholic Church celebrates Mass according to the Latin

Rite, it refers near the centre of its most solemn prayer to 'the sacrifice of our father Abraham', *sacrificium Patriarchae nostri Abrahae*. All that we have learned in the last fifty years, especially in new religious understanding and a more critical sense of one's own history, has really only revivified this basic original consciousness of a shared tradition of revelation and belief, of prayer, of a way of seeing the divine concern with humanity. If one consciously shares in that tradition, one cannot regard oneself as simply an outsider to Jewish experience. It remains a relationship of cousinship. Jewish identity has survived less through blood than through belief and practice, a consciousness rooted in spiritual commitment to a recognisable view of humanity and divinity. To a quite considerable extent a Christian must share in that commitment. It is at least in that mind that I would speak to the two issues I have outlined.

First the relationship of Judaism to the State of Israel. It would seem that the religious tradition which looks back to Abraham has in its essentials through most of its history stood remarkably free of the political, free not in being apolitical but in being well above the political. A great monotheist tradition must, indeed, be so. It cannot be tied down, or morally confined to, the limitations of a single state. It was for centuries at home in most parts of Europe, in the France of Rashi, the Spain of Nahmanides, the eastern Europe of Hasidism, just as Abraham and Isaac were at home as nomads in the ancient middle east, or their descendants at home in the Egypt of Joseph's Pharaoh, even in Babylon where Jeremiah had urged the first exiles to build houses and live in them, plant gardens and eat their produce, where the Talmud was later written. Of course, there was always the fear of persecution and the hope of return, yet every time there was a return to Jerusalem, there was also a new failure to attain the high moral demands of Yahweh, a new state of sin. In a historical religion there cannot be an achieved state of perfection but only a constant oscillation between good and evil and also, in the tradition of Israel, between holy city and exile. Exile may be the consequence of sin but it also manifests the inherent universalism of Mosaic monotheism. If Jeremiah sees in a vision two baskets of figs, one very good figs, the other very bad figs, and the very good figs are the exiles from Judah, the very bad figs the king, the princes, those who remain, this is not a vision inapplicable beyond the sixth century. Kings and cities, priests and prophets, come and go, but the worship of true God with a contrite heart and humble spirit by any believer anywhere continues unbroken.

That vision of Jeremiah is at the culmination of a long prophetic critique of the state beginning with Nathan's parable to David, Elijah's denunciation of the murder of Naboth and expropriation of his vineyard, the book of Amos. What has proved world shattering and forever relevant in Israel's tradition of theism was precisely this, that faith in Yahweh had such wide and seemingly secular requirements: love, justice, but most strikingly a critique of the treatment of the weak by contemporary political power, Israelite power especially. It is in its ability for national self-criticism, dependent upon a prophetic distancing from state control but not from public concern, that it shaped a religious tradition which has remained one of our perishable earth's most valuable possessions and, I may add, one of Christianity's most blessed inheritances. Thus, if Archbishop Carey or Cardinal Hume feel compelled to criticise uncaring government policy, it is basically because they are children of Abraham and heirs in some share to the spirit of Nathan, Elijah and Amos.

I have not the slightest doubt that that spirit is alive in Israel today, the refusal among many Israelis to accept as consonant with the claims of Yahweh any sort of politico-religious justification for social injustice, for a renewed expropriation of Naboth's vineyard. But there too, as in any dominantly Christian country in which the church shares power in some form of establishment, there is inevitably a strong tendency as well to go along with, close one's eyes to, justify, the ill-treatment of the weak by government or by religious fanatics. It would be miraculous if it were not so, and it would be quite out of line with what we are led to expect by the Hebrew scriptures. They do and always will remain our prime tool of spiritual interpretation for contemporary politics. But the distancing from the state in its hard contemporary reality which the prophets achieved and which was indeed implicit in the whole development of Hebraic religion, also made the survival of the Jewish community very much more possible outside Palestine and in a world diaspora which would continue from then until now. The Hebrew religious tradition and its principal immediate bearer, the Jewish community, could no longer be confined to a small geographical area. The diaspora was, essentially, not a mistake or a disaster or even a mere temporary divine punishment, it was a right and inevitable consequence – at both religious and secular levels – of Judaism being what it was. It was, of course, by no means reversed by the Return in the ages of Nehemiah and Ezra.

It is incontrovertible that the scriptural side of the tradition concentrated upon the community in Jerusalem and the expectation of return, but it is no less indisputable that the reality of Jewish religious experience has been far wider than that. It was in fact within the context of the diaspora that Judaism, the post-biblical religion as we know it, was developed. It is, I would suggest, through the sustained interaction of diaspora and holy city, of universalism and particularism, of the multiplicity of synagogue and the uniqueness of temple, that the tradition as a whole has been definitively shaped. Sacred literature may have focused upon the second pole but the vitality and sheer survival of the tradition have depended far more upon the former. The synagogue can be anywhere, the temple only in Jerusalem, but it is upon the synagogue not upon the temple that in reality post-biblical Judaism has been focused, much as the Bible speaks of temple and not of synagogue.

The establishment of the modern state of Israel, its intrinsic need to increase its population, together with the profound fear created by the Holocaust, have all contributed in our time to create a new agenda and to place a question mark against any justification for diaspora Judaism. Between the pressures of assimilation and the pressures for Return, the very existence of Judaism outside Israel may seem today uncertain. One can seriously ask whether in another couple of generations Judaism will even exist, at least in Europe, apart from a minimal presence in a few capital cities, and Jews may well ask themselves, Is there any real reason why it should survive outside Israel? Yet I believe that if it does not, Hitler will in a way have triumphed. The call of the Return must be almost agonisingly strong for many Jews but I am convinced that the survival of Judaism outside Israel is not to be seen in terms of worldliness, of any mere reluctance of Jews to give up their way of life elsewhere to participate in building up the young state, but in a deeper logic within Judaism itself, a rich dialectic within the central thread of biblical and post-biblical religious experience. The disappearance of Judaism outside Israel could constitute an abandonment of one of the very poles of that experience, the moral requirement to stand prophetically apart from the political state, to survive without it, and to provide a universal witness. Moreover the rest of the world needs this pole of your tradition, and Europe, which has so long both used and abused you, needs it most particularly. We may now say with all our hearts, as did the Falasha to Gabra Masih, 'Stay with me in your manner', but if Jews reply with the Abuna 'I wish to join with my brothers', what complaint can we make? Yet for Europe it would truly be devastating, at this moment of its post-Cold War reconstruction, to be wholly deprived of one of its most ancient and most formative national traditions, for such in truth you are.

If we are convinced that the Jewish community, the household of Judaism, must not, and therefore will not, shrink geographically to be confined within the frontiers of the state of Israel, the conviction needs nevertheless to be derived from a Judaic rather than a European logic. If so it is vitally necessary to think afresh about the religious role of the diaspora community in an age when the State of Israel does exist, and has now developed into a powerful, essentially secular, political reality, possessing and using guns, bombs, prisons. The authentic voice of religious authority has of necessity to remain distinct from the voice of prime ministers and of generals, but this is simply not a problem which had to be faced by Jews until recently, much as it has had to be faced by Christians. It is one that it may be, at least, sometimes easier to face if all Jews are not in the same country – just as it can be easier for Christians to face it when not confined within a national established church. A prophetic voice outside Israel is not a substitute for a prophetic voice within Israel but the one may stimulate the other. Thus for many of us outsiders, the declaration of the Chief Rabbi of Britain, Lord Jakobovits, that the Palestinian refugee camps are 'a stain on humanity – people locked up in those wretched camps for forty years. We ought to cry out to the world, we ought not to wait until terrorists draw attention to this', was immensely important, coming from whom it did, precisely as an example of the moral role appropriate to world Judaism *vis à vis* Israel. But the Jewish prophetic voice in this country and in Europe is needed no less urgently in regard to our own problems. New threats of racialism can be heard on every side and many immigrant communities are being subject to increasing harassment and discrimination upon the continent. The Jews are elder brothers of every harassed racial minority, and their voice is greatly needed in today's Europe both to oppose racialism and to give witness to the need for a pluralism of races and of beliefs within a single continent as part of Europe's own historic tradition and a condition for all true human peace.

The contribution of the Jewish community to wider society has never been a merely religious one and it certainly should not be now. Nevertheless, part of it should surely be religious and for this not to be so would seem almost a betrayal of its central sustaining principle. Again, if there is to be a religious Jewish contribution to a wider wisdom achieved through the interpretation, vindication and application of Judaism in and to our common world, then that must be done to a considerable extent within universities. It does of course need its own institutions too, but it needs also to participate in such institutions of the wider society as are genuinely open and accessible to it. In the United States this has long been obvious. Most major universities have their departments of Judaism or of Jewish Studies, or their Jewish participants in departments of Religious Studies. In Britain, at least until recently, this has hardly been the case. Jews have, undoubtedly, been represented with great distinction in most fields of study within British universities other than theology and religious studies. Much the same was true until twenty years ago of Roman Catholics. Developments in the last few years at Oxford, at the Centre for Hebrew Studies, and at University College, London, are major breaks in this pattern and there have been smaller ones elsewhere, for instance in the establishment at Birmingham of the Centre for the Study of Judaism and Jewish/Christian Relations. I feel sure, nevertheless, that there is still considerable room for development of a larger presence of Judaism within British departments of Religious Studies.

Thirty years ago, such departments hardly existed. What did exist were Anglican and/or Protestant Theological Faculties geared fairly closely to the education of ordinands for Christian churches other than the Roman Catholic. The opening up of this whole field from theology to a large concern with religious studies, from Anglican domination to a genuinely ecumenical academic community, is a development which now makes it fully possible for believing Jews to enter in, both to learn and to teach. To leave out post-biblical Judaism where Islam, Hinduism or Buddhism is studied is to maim the study of religion itself. The presence of Judaism in the university syllabus can only be of great value for non-Jews and for the British academic field in general, but what I have been trying to suggest is that it is important too from a specifically Jewish viewpoint, as part of a determination not to limit Jewish presence in the world, or the influence of Judaism, to the State of Israel, important as the latter obviously must be for that presence and influence. It is in terms of the intrinsic logic of Judaism, I would claim, that such a refusal needs to be made and in no way should it be seen as inimical to the State of Israel. Quite the contrary. It is simply part of recognition that in religious and human terms the presence and influence of Judaism in God's world should not be confined nationalistically to a single state and that the very internationalism of Jewish experience and of Judaism over the centuries is something not to be lost. It is, moreover, something which may particularly help to cherish the prophetic element within the biblical tradition, the freedom of religion to criticise the state in the name of God, for the sake of justice and the protection of the oppressed.

It would for Great Britain be sad if the Anglo–Jewish community was simply to fade away in the coming decades, but it would, I believe, be no less sad for Judaism itself. The same is true for Europe. But beyond any specific region or cultural area, Judaism has long had a universalist vocation which it can only fulfil in the condition of being present as a minority unprotected by its own political force. Survival will depend not on inertia but on a positive sense of religious purpose. And if survival outside Israel may be a risk, it is also a God-given privilege. The people of God in this world, people that is to say consciously trying to assert a vision and a morality of love, compassion, hospitality, justice, because such things reflect the very nature of the God we cannot see, should not fear to be a minority, and they always will be. They will still be the salt of the earth.

**A lecture given to the Fellowship of Christians and Jews, Leeds,
October 1991**

NOTES

1   Stephen Kaplan, 'The Fälasha and the Stephanite: An Episode from *Gädlä Gäbrä Mäsih*', *Bulletin of the School of Oriental and African Studies*, XLVII (1985), p. 282.

14

Guilt

The meaning of guilt is unintelligible without the recognition of its inbuilt ambiguity. It relates to crime upon the one hand, sin upon the other. These are, without question, overlapping realities, yet they overlap far less than one's initial impression might suggest. They are in fact deeply different, tied awkwardly together by a shared link with guilt. Let me begin by relating guilt to crime. After that I will turn to sin. Finally I will try to outline the problems in an understanding of guilt which includes both. We still tend too easily, as society in the past often tended, to identify the two. Perhaps we willingly distinguish them in theory yet still in practice adopt a sort of shorthand approach which equates one to the other. Instead we need to follow through the logic of their difference in the way we approach both crime and the criminal.

By crime I mean a conscious breaking of the law of the state. Now it is obvious that no political society could function without laws. Given human beings as they are, laws are inconceivable without a measure of lawbreaking, law-enforcement, forms of police, forms of punishment. Courts, police and prisons all relate to crime. The concept of crime conceals all sorts of complexities. Nevertheless, there is a hard reality to it and the deliberate breaking of a positive law is a clear enough concept. Crime is, in a sense, an inevitable part of the functioning of every society known to us in history, though there has certainly been far more crime in some societies than in others. That may depend upon how far a society is legally structured in a way that is fair to all its members and expressive of a shared culture. But crime exists even in the best societies and with it the concept of guilt. Guilt adds to crime the dimension of consciousness, the awareness of responsibility for lawbreaking. Every civilised legal system recognises that crime is more than the objective breaking of a law, it involves too an element of awareness, of intention.

Guilt plainly does not depend upon its demonstration. Nevertheless, from the viewpoint of a legal system what really matters is not guilt but proven guilt. That is true in police terms, in newspaper terms, in libel terms but not in moral terms. If adequate evidence is not available to a court, a murderer is no less guilty, but you may not say that he is guilty. If someone is acquitted, it certainly does not mean that she or he is not guilty. It says something about a legal process, not about what happened in the event which provoked the legal process. What we can be quite sure of is that many people are acquitted when they are guilty and some people are convicted when they are innocent. Publicly one can only follow the judgement in a trial, though in some cases we may have the greatest doubt as to its reliability or even the competence of a judge. While there can be no alternative to functioning in this way, what matters to us here is the considerable gap it already establishes between the officially, legally, guilty and the truly guilty even with reference to specific legal crimes. The lack of one additional witness, the presence of one perjured witness, may make all the difference – to conviction but not to guilt.

Beyond all the cases of wrong judgement are the surely far more numerous ones of guilty people who are never brought to trial. We know what a small proportion of crimes in Britain, crimes of violence and of theft, ever lead to an arrest. Those guilty of these crimes are all around us. But one can think too of kinds of crime and other groups of people, particularly among the very rich and powerful, where it can be extraordinarily difficult even to suggest guilt. No one can have any doubt about the scale and variety of Robert Maxwell's crimes, but I wonder very much whether we would know about them now were he not dead. The power of wealth in our society to intimidate, to conceal, to undermine the legal structure of society is now enormous and it is constantly used. The very internationality of the economic community, the existence of tax havens, the diversity of laws, all make the undermining of any real rule of law extremely easy for the rich, the clever and the unscrupulous. Maxwell was certainly not unique. Moreover, the close interlocking of the politically powerful and the commercially powerful, the easy way in which people now move from the one world to the other so soon as they are out of the Cabinet, makes this even more serious. There is a very murky area of guilt here at the heart of our society, near to the actual controlling mechanisms of the rule of law, where guilt will very seldom be established except perhaps in retrospect.

Let us now turn to our other pole of meaning – sin. By this I mean behaviour, personal or collective, which we recognise as morally wicked, unethical, an affront to the nature and goodness of God, something which has an objectivity of evil quite apart from any positive law. It is an intrinsic offence against the moral order.

I suspect that there is almost no one who does not employ the concept of guilt with reference to things which are not seen as crimes in this, or, indeed, any state. Some of them, particularly certain sexual offences, may be judged to be crimes in certain Islamic countries. While most of us do not agree with that, we do not deny that many of these matters genuinely involve guilt. The first thing to be clear about is, then, that the area of moral guilt is far larger than that of crime-related guilt. In themselves drunkenness, a vile temper, lying, bullying of many sorts, are not things which it is practical or desirable to make the subject of positive state law, yet when one considers their effect upon others, and the moral corruption involved in a consistent and perhaps deliberate indulgence in such behaviour, we are certainly right to relate to such behaviour the idea of guilt.

Most of us take for granted the difference between those two sorts of guilt though we use a single word to cover them; most of us, moreover, would regard moral guilt as something more reprehensible than legal guilt. Indeed we see the latter as really reprehensible only when we judge it to partake of the former. Thus we may remark that so and so has broken the law but most of the guilt really lies with the parents, or society, the way a young person has been brought up over the years. Yet we recognise that the guilt of the parents may not include ever having actually broken any law of the land. Minor but persistent domestic cruelty, alcoholism, lying can never as such be made into illegal behaviour, yet there may be far more guilt in such things – at least as most of us see it – than in many actions which do break the criminal law. Guilt is, in fact, primarily a moral category and only because this already exists is it really possible to carry it over into the field of state law. Yet the relationship between the two remains far from clear. Traditional Christian theology of a Catholic kind links the two through the concept of 'natural law' and the obligation of positive law to base itself upon natural law. Positive law becomes some sort of embodiment, suitable to a specific society, of the obligations of natural law. Undoubtedly a theory of natural law raises considerable problems of various sorts, but I do not myself believe that we can dispense with it even though the cultural perception in different societies as to what is moral and what immoral does vary profoundly. It varies, of course, even within a single society.

The British perception about the basic morality of, for instance, killing as a punishment for crime has altered hugely. Two hundred years ago most people, from bishops down, thought it right to hang their neighbours for theft. Very few of us would today think that anything but abhorrent. Forty years ago most British people were happy with capital punishment as the normal sentence for murder. While our society is still divided over this, the weight of thoughtful opinion has shifted enormously. Over the destruction of pre-birth human life through abortion, we find ourselves profoundly divided in our moral perceptions. Some people are utterly convinced, with a great weight of tradition behind them, that those responsible for abortions are very guilty – not necessarily against civil law, but against the ultimately unchanging principles of basic morality. Others strongly disagree. While it is important to note such deep divergences, it may be that in their way even such disagreements still witness to the main thesis: the reality of moral guilt. Those people who do not care to locate it in one area of human activity appear more or less compelled to do so in another.

Note too that it is not the case that one necessarily thinks that all the more serious cases of breaking the moral law are taken up by state law and only minor infringements are left to the moral law only. It is a far more complex matter than that. There may be far more real guilt in some of the things that the civil law does not, and rightly does not, take up than in some of the things which it does. State law takes them up on grounds of public utility far more than on grounds of moral seriousness.

Nevertheless at the end of it all, when we think and speak of the guilty, we seldom specify very precisely whether we mean moral guilt or legal guilt. We continue at least to use the same word despite the fact that, while in some cases there is a large measure of overlap between the two, in others there is little or none. Moreover the division between the two is not as such between the private and the public. Gross misuse of wealth and political power are matters of public guilt whether or not they involve the formally illegal. Cabinet ministers and leading civil servants who systematically deceive both Parliament and the public are to be judged guilty in the public domain. When one considers, to take just one example, the duplicity and profound evasiveness of those responsible in the 'arms for Iraq' affair, as revealed by the Scott Commission, it is hard not to agree to that. We are thinking of matters over which ministers would certainly have resigned in an earlier, more honourable age. The guilt involved in such deceptions may be far greater in both moral and public terms than that of many people sent to prison for small dishonesties.

Hitherto we have been presuming that the category of crime does at least fall within the category of the immoral even if the two areas weigh seriousness rather differently. But we have now to go a step further and recognise that many laws of modern states, as of states in the past, are in fact actually wicked. The race laws of Nazi Germany were an obvious example but so, to come still closer to the present and to a country functioning quite comparably to our own, was many a law of apartheid South Africa. A British prison chaplain could well have moved to South Africa and taken up a post in its prison service. There a person of one race marrying someone of another was breaking the law and would be sent to prison. Many of us know South African couples, black and white, who have had to flee from their country because by marrying they were law breakers. To look somewhat further back in our own society many prison chaplains in Queen Elizabeth II's prison service would have been guilty of a crime punishable by death in the England of Elizabeth I, simply by virtue of the fact that they were ordained Roman Catholic priests and had celebrated Mass.

My father was a lawyer and a judge and had been brought up in the positivist legal tradition of England. I remember his insisting that in principle the law had nothing to do with justice. Law depended upon Parliament. If Parliament declared that every blue-eyed baby should be killed, then that would be the law of the land. Against that I appealed to the medieval conception of law as valid only if it reflected the natural and divine law. There was once a tradition of legal understanding in this country upheld by lawyers like Bracton and Coke which grounded it in morality but it has long ceased to be, although in the rhetoric of those denouncing crime that is generally overlooked. Constitutionally Britain, without any Bill of Rights, is an extreme and explicit case of the gap between morality and law which to some extent exists in every country in the world. Every use of the word 'justice' in relation to the enforcement of the law is in consequence inherently equivocal. Law enforcers, when they talk about guilt in relation to crime, want to be able to count upon the moral pressure of guilt in relation to sin, but law makers in the business of enlarging their prerogative have in principle denied the connection.

Even when a crime appears objectively to fall within the category of sin, the moral law may well recognise, notably in the taking of goods in cases of real need, that it is in the circumstances justified. A basic community of goods and the right of the very poor to help themselves in need are reiterated parts of the patristic moral tradition, but they can hardly be included within a code of positive law.

A newspaper cutting which I have always cherished, dated 22 November 1975, is headed 'Woman Who Stole 36 Pence Must Go To Prison'. It tells of a woman who stole 36 pence and was jailed at Shrewsbury Crown Court for nine months after the court was told that no National Health Service hospital was prepared to accept her as a patient. Mrs Smith had stolen 36 pence from another lodger's purse at a County Council hostel. As the defence lawyer said 'It's utterly ridiculous that a person should be imprisoned for stealing 36 pence when their intelligence level places them little above the moronic. She only just knows what she is doing.' But the prosecution obtained a conviction. The absolute meaninglessness of this conviction in moral terms for a person of her intelligence should be obvious. I kept the cutting really because, whether deliberately or not, the newspaper had printed exactly on the reverse another story entitled 'Woman With Four Fur Coats Gets Legal Aid!' Whether anyone else noted this I do not know but I chanced to do so and I cut it out. I have always cherished it and I look at it from time to time because it is indicative of the extraordinary way our legal system can work and its relation to both class and guilt. Of course, if you have four fur coats and all that goes with four fur coats you can very often play the legal system in a way that, if you need 36 pence, you cannot. So, although both were found guilty, the woman with four fur coats was given a fine which she paid straight away while the woman who stole 36 pence was sent to prison.

When we have considered so many different kinds of case, the gap between the two types of guilt must be clear enough, and yet the problem remains that the enforcement of the criminal law appears to require as much pressure as it can obtain from the moral law if it is to have any chance of success. As the sense of any clear moral authority, Christian or other, declines in this country, so the general willingness to break the law when it seems convenient to do so grows larger and larger, to the general damage of society. Here as elsewhere the contradictory stance of the leadership of our society towards the moral nature of law, long present but now perhaps more evident than in the past, is proving profoundly destructive of its health.

I have been speaking hitherto about the difference between two sorts of guilt in rather objective terms but, of course, subjectivities keep breaking in – the low-level guilt consciousness in the woman who stole 36 pence, the high level of moral commitment in a friend of mine who refused to pay her poll tax as a protest against its being far too low for a person of her wealth, the love of the mixed race couple who have fled South Africa. Guilt is not just a matter of awareness of having broken a law, it relates to the total moral consciousness of the person in question. It is a psychological state. Some people have a profound, indeed exaggerated, sense of guilt; some appear to have almost none at all. People with a strong sense of it may feel guilty about the smallest things, or simply because they have done nothing when they see in retrospect that they could have acted to prevent some misfortune: someone was in need and they did not extend the help they might have done. Some people can tear themselves to pieces both mentally and physically because they feel so guilty, while other people can commit almost any offence without, so far as one can see, feeling the slightest remorse about it. Due recognition of one's own guiltiness here depends upon the formation of what traditional Catholic moral theology called a sound conscience, the ability to evaluate one's behaviour in moral terms without being irrationally overwhelmed by it. Subjectively guilt, especially bouts of an intense feeling of guilt, can be something felt far more with hindsight than at the time. There are things we do, but feel next to no immediate remorse. Years later a sense of guilt about them may suddenly become almost overwhelming. In his Confessions, Augustine analyses the sins of his youth, including the famous incident when he stole some pears: 'So small a child, so big a sinner.' Most of us, reading the Confessions, may feel that Augustine exaggerated the guilt and the degree of sinfulness involved. Probably he did not feel so guilty at the time. The pastoral care of the guilty has to be related more to the subjective condition than to the objective action. It can need to counter among some a still surviving Augustinian influence with too great a sense of guilt just as much as to get others to recognise the reality of being guilty.

Having surveyed the whole wide range of guilt and its different forms, in which there are people who are judged legally guilty whom we would say for all sorts of different reasons are in a deeper sense not guilty or hardly guilty, while so many other people are very guilty yet not legally so, we have finally to ask: Are any of us not guilty? The straight answer is 'No'. Guilt is a reality in which in one way or another everyone is involved. That is a fact of life. It is also part of Christian doctrine. There is a human community of guilt, far beyond the realms of proven legal crime. At the end of it all we need to recognise that it is an inevitable part of our moral being as humans that we are sinners, sharing every one of us in a quality of guiltiness. Perhaps we can only help people to cope with guilt if, first of all, we can agree on that. We may then go on to make some sense of the diversities of guilt, and, of course, accept that some guilts are much more publicly serious or more morally destructive than others, but it is from within a community of the guilty that we have to approach guilt, not as people who stand outside or think that it is even possible to stand outside. There is no us and them. We must come, all of us, as publicans not as pharisees. If we do so we may need to proclaim rather different standards of guiltiness from those presented by the law, by society or even by the church. Outside prison, as much as within it, there is a full range of guilt. Perhaps that is true even within the ranks of the clergy. In our ministry it may be no less important to point to the guiltiness of those outside prison as to help cope with the guiltiness of some of those within, and the one could be a key to the other. Yet, if guilt is pervasive and largely immeasurable, it can never be the end of the story. Maybe it is only when someone recognises that he or she personally participates in a community of guilt that the gospel analysis of sin, a divine Saviour and the offer of a forgiveness none of us can merit, begins to make some sense. We may then be empowered to help others discover another community far beyond guilt, a community of the genuinely humane, of hope, of forgiveness, of love. Theologically, the universality of guilt is but the backdrop to the universality of forgiveness. Perhaps in practice it is when we recognise convincingly the reality of the first that we can become credible guides to the reality of the second.

**A paper given at the Prison Chaplains' Conference, Leeds,
29 September 1993**

15

The Prince of Peace

At first sight the account of Jesus' messianic entry into Jerusalem riding upon an ass (Matt 25:5) may not seem to have much to do with Christmas. Yet I think it has, especially when we focus our attention first upon the ass. I knew of some people who lived in Khartoum in the old days of British rule. Independence and the time for them to leave was approaching. Their little son, who had frequently been taken for walks past the great statue of Gordon mounted on a camel, begged to be taken once more to say goodbye: he was immensely devoted to Gordon. As they turned away he asked his mother, tears of parting in his eyes, 'Mummy, who is that man on Gordon's back?'.

I am not wanting to suggest that only the animal matters and not the rider; rather, that we need here to consider an almost symbiotic relationship between the two. The ass tells us a lot about Jesus; and Jesus, too, tells us a lot about the ass. The choice of an ass was not accidental, as the prophetic text of Zechariah (9:9) makes clear: Rejoice, daughter of Zion, shout aloud, daughter of Jerusalem; for see, your king is coming to you, his cause won, his victory gained, humble and mounted on an ass. . . . He shall banish chariots and war-horses, the warrior's bow, tanks, submarines, nuclear rockets; he shall speak peaceably to every nation.

But why an ass? The ass or donkey is a gentle, insignificant, serviceable animal, 'a dull, stupid fellow', *Chambers Dictionary* tells us, all the difference in the world from the noble horse who is the true princely companion, depicted in so many royal portraits. If Zechariah's prince was to banish the war-horse, he would be depriving the royals of a great deal of fun, for the cavalry charge was the quintessential thrill of upper-class war. All very different from the appropriate expectations raised by a man on a donkey.

His meaning, and the donkey's meaning, is of a serviceable, domesticated pacifism, a paradise for the common man. The ass indeed has two memorable hours in biblical history: in one she bore Jesus into Jerusalem in a sort of poignant parody of secular power; in the other, a long time earlier, she had carried Balaam and been privileged to be the one animal permitted to speak – and how very sensible her remarks were. A worried little politician faced with an invasion of immigrants, Balak, had wanted priestly support to curse these aliens. He called in Balaam. Balaam, so far as we can guess, while he knew pretty clearly that he should not go along with Balak, was in some danger of doing so all the same. Hence the angel with the fiery sword which his ass, this dull, stupid fellow, saw in the way. He swerved to avoid it. Balaam, who saw nothing, said angrily to the animal, 'If I had a sword, I'd kill you on the spot'. 'Am I not still the ass which you have ridden all your life?', the animal gently replied. 'Can't you see what I am endeavouring to avoid?' Then Balaam did see and instead of going along with Balak and cursing Israel, he instead pronounced blessings: blessings and peace.

Jesus on his ass entered Jerusalem to bring the sort of peace which Balaam on his ass had also brought in that very ancient story. It was not what the contemporary leaders in Jerusalem wanted any more than it was what Balak wanted.

The Christmas mythology is very, and rightly, strong on the ox and the ass. It is true that the gospels do not mention them but they mention the manger, which is quite enough.

> A manger was the cradle
> That Christ was rocked in,
> The provender the asses left
> So sweetly he slept on.[1]

Jesus is, I think, rather like the protofigure in some African clan genealogy, born together with an animal – crocodile, buck or lion – and thus establishing a permanent totemic relationship with his half-brother, human with animal. Borne by the ass on which he will ride in mock triumph as a prince of peace, he becomes that sort of prince who can appropriately ride on an ass, and this is the sort of peace to which we aspire in the celebration of Christmas: a peace in which humanity humbly rediscovers kinship with the animal creation (remember the old myth that on Christmas night all the animals can speak in human tongues), an animal world over which it has ridden with no dialogue whatsoever till danger stands across the road. It is the ass, this dull, stupid fellow, who tells us what an unaggressive kingdom of peace must be all about. And that, perhaps, is the message of Christmas.

A Christmas sermon preached in the University of Leeds
December 1989

NOTES

1 'The Carnal and the Crane', *Oxford Book of Carols*.

Further Reading

Duncan Forrester, *Theology and Politics* (Blackwell, 1988) and Ronald Preston, *Church and Society in the Late Twentieth Century: The Economic and Political Task* (SCM, 1983), provide two ways into the discussion about how to relate Christian life, theology, politics and prophecy. See also John Macquarrie's beautiful little *The Concept of Peace* (SCM, 1973 and 1990) and Robin Gill, *Prophecy and Praxis: The Social Function of the Churches* (Marshall, Morgan and Scott, 1981).

Valuable background books include K. Medhurst and G. Moyser, *Church and Politics in a Secular Age* (Oxford, 1988), G. Moyser (ed.), *Church and Politics Today: The Role of the Church of England in Contemporary Politics* (T & T Clark, 1985), G. Moyser (ed.), *Politics and Religion in the Modern World* (Routledge, 1991) and A. Hastings, *A History of English Christianity 1920–1990* (SCM, 1990).

Robin Gill, *A Textbook of Christian Ethics* (T & T Clark, 1985) provides a great deal of material formative of the tradition of Christian morality. Donald MacKinnon, *Explorations in Theology 5* (SCM, 1979) is a set of essays by one of the greatest – if frequently obscure – practitioners of the last generation, and Rosino Gibellini, *The Liberation Theology Debate* (SCM, 1987) a helpful introduction to one of the most influential contemporary approaches, together with its Roman critique. David Jenkins, *God, Politics and the Future* (SCM, 1988) is a collection of sermons and addresses by a bishop who is certainly also a theologian and, possibly, also a prophet.

William Temple's *Christianity and Social Order* (a Penguin Special, 1942) was republished in 1976 with a foreword by Edward Heath and introduction by Ronald Preston. For the significance of Bell, see Kenneth Slack, *George Bell* (SCM, 1971) and Peter Walker, *Rediscovering the Middle Way: The Anglican Church Today* (Mowbray, 1988). Eberhard

Bethge, *Dietrich Bonhoeffer* (Collins, 1970) is the standard biography of one of the greatest prophets of our century but see also Edwin Robertson, *The Shame and the Sacrifice: The Life and Teaching of Dietrich Bonhoeffer* (Hodder, 1987) and Renate Wind, *A Spoke in the Wheel* (SCM, 1991) a briefer study.

For a much-discussed, if not too coherent, counter-voice to most of the books listed hitherto, see Edward Norman, *Church and Society in England 1770–1970* (Oxford, 1976) and his Reith Lectures, *Christianity and the World Order* (Oxford, 1979). The former, lengthy and academic, the latter, brief and populist, share an underlying purpose to denounce what their author sees as 'the politicization of Christianity'. Three sets of replies to the Reith Lectures may be noted: Haddon Willmer (ed.), *Christian Faith and Political Hopes*, (Epworth, 1979), Michael Dummett, *Catholicism and World Order* (Catholic Institute of International Relations, 1979) and Eric James (ed.), *Christian Action Journal*, (Spring 1979). For a massively learned and somewhat idiosyncratic work sympathetic, at least in part, to the Norman stance, see the two volumes of Maurice Cowling, *Religion and Public Doctrine in Modern England*, (Cambridge, 1980 and 1985). Chapter 14 of volume I discusses Norman together with Enoch Powell.

Three sources of lively booklets on issues of church and society should also be noted. The Catholic Institute of International Relations has published a range of pamphlets including *Eucharist and Politics* by Thomas Cullinan, OSB and Ian Linden's recent *Back to Basics* (1994). The Centre for Theology and Public Issues of the University of Edinburgh publishes a series of Occasional Papers, including no. 23, *Vision and Prophecy: The Tasks of Social Theology Today* (1991). The Board of Social Responsibility of the Church of England produces a range of reports, such as *Not Just for the Poor: Christian Perspectives on the Welfare State* (Church House Publishing, 1986). A well-argued critique of the Board's publications can be found in Henry Clark, *The Church under Thatcher* (SPCK, 1993).

Finally, some other books of mine which tie in with our main theme. A chapter on prophecy (pp. 54–68) of *The Theology of a Protestant Catholic* (SCM, 1990) discusses its contemporary meaning and role more formally than I do here. *Church and the State: the English Experience* (University of Exeter Press, 1991) underlies Chapter 9. *The Faces of God* (Geoffrey Chapman, 1975), *In Filial Disobedience* (Mayhew-McCrimmon, 1978), *In the Hurricane* (Collins, 1986) and *The Theology of a Protestant Catholic* all explore in an undeniably personal but also public way the interface of Truth, Church and Society. *Wiriyamu* (Search Press, 1974) and *SOS Bosnia* (The Alliance to Defend Bosnia-Herzegovina, three editions, 1993 and 1994) underlie chapters 12 and 13.

Name Index